THE USAAF
1926–45

Training for war – magnificent flight of Model 75 PT-13 Stearmans, 1936. The PT-13 was the first in a long line of primary 'Kaydet' trainers, the Army placing its first Stearman order for twenty-six PT-13s in July 1935. The production PT-13 flew for the first time in April 1936, and deliveries were made between June and December 1936. Stearman operated from Wichita, Kansas, until 1 April 1938 when Boeing Aircraft acquired the company and created its Stearman Aircraft Division.

Boeing

THE USAAF
1926–45

MARTIN W. BOWMAN

SUTTON PUBLISHING

First published in 2000 by
Sutton Publishing Limited · Phoenix Mill
Thrupp · Stroud · Gloucestershire · GL5 2BU

British Library Cataloguing in Publication Data
A catalogue record for this book is available from the British Library

ISBN 0 7509 2461 5

Background photograph: Cold and callous. During the Second World War USAAF bomber crews sometimes lost men and machines through their own mistakes. Here, one of a stick of 1,000-lb bombs dropped from a B-17 of the 94th Bomb Group, 8th Air Force, over Berlin on 19 May 1944 has knocked off the left horizontal stabilizer of 42-31540 *Miss Donna Mae* of the 331st Bomb Squadron below. This B-17G went into an uncontrollable spin and at 13,000 ft the wing broke off and the Fortress spun crazily to the ground. There were no survivors.

USAF

Typeset in 11/15 pt Baskerville.
Typesetting and origination by
Sutton Publishing Limited.
Printed and bound in England by
J.H. Haynes & Co. Ltd, Sparkford.

INTRODUCTION

When the USA entered the First World War on 6 April 1917 her military air services and aircraft industry were in an even more parlous state than that of most of the European powers in 1914. The Army Aviation Service had only about 300 aircraft, none of which were suitable for combat on the Western Front, so the British-designed de Havilland 4 (DH4) became the standard combat aircraft. Several other British and French types were also used, the most famous being the SPAD and Sopwith Camel. After the war the USA Army quickly demobilized most of its air arm and little progress was made in military aviation in the peacetime service.

During the isolationist period between the two world wars the USA relied on a small peacetime organization that would be capable of rapid expansion in war. On 4 June 1920 an Air Service was created as a combatant arm of the USA Army. The Air Corps Act of 2 July 1926 initiated a five-year expansion programme for 1,514 officers, 16,000 EM and 1,800 serviceable aircraft. Between 1927 and 1932 just eight new groups were activated. Five of them were pursuit, with one observation. The standard bomber from 1928 to 1932 was the Keystone series, closely followed by the Curtiss B-2 Condor. The Keystone could only manage speeds of just over 100mph and the Condor's performance was less. Significantly, only two of the eight new groups in Army service between 1928 and 1932 were bombardment.

On 1 March 1935 the War Department established General Headquarters Air Force (GHQAF) to serve as an air defence and striking force, and an air officer was at last appointed to command. Some observation units remained assigned to corps areas, but all the pursuit, bombardment and attack units in the USA became part of the new combat organization. The change of the 9th Group from observation to bombardment in 1935 and the inactivation of the 12th Observation Group in 1937 finally signalled the decline in observation and the growth of bombardment aviation.

During the 1930s the accepted theory was that a formation of unescorted bombers could get through to their target if they were properly arranged and armed sufficiently. After air manoeuvres in 1933 Brigadier-General Oscar Westover had wanted to eliminate pursuits altogether because of their repeated failure to intercept the bombers. As the 1940s dawned, senior USAAC officers believed that air power could directly influence the course of future wars by having strategic air forces fly long-range missions and destroy an enemy's industrial infrastructure. However, funds for new aircraft were very limited and it was often left to manufacturers to fund their own developments in the hope that they would in turn attract orders from the Army.

By late 1938 the USA Army Air Corps (USAAC) had a strength of just 1,600 aircraft and production was only fractionally above 88 planes a month. In January 1939 Roosevelt asked Congress to strengthen the USA's air power, which the President said was 'utterly inadequate'. In April 1939 Congress finally passed the expansion bill authorizing the Air Corps ceiling of 5,500 aircraft. On 1 September 1939 Hitler attacked Poland, and the Second World War began. America had two years' breathing space before she too entered the global war. In the meantime, industry geared up to build the new aircraft whose technical development was improved by the hard won experience gained by the RAF in combat in Europe. In June 1941 a new, autonomous Army division, the Army Air Forces (AAF), was created under the command of Major-General Henry H. 'Hap' Arnold.

The USA was thrust headlong into the Second World War by the Japanese air attack on Pearl Harbor on 7 December 1941, and the following day Germany declared war on the USA. Arnold and his staff now formulated a policy of relentless air attacks against Germany, strategic defence in the Pacific theatre and air operations in the defence of the western hemisphere.

The USAAF was to fight a global war, from Alaska to the Pacific, the Mediterranean, North Africa and Italy, and from Great Britain. In Europe US air forces helped secure total victory. The Germans in Italy surrendered on 29 April 1945 and on 7 May Germany unconditionally surrendered to the Allies; 8 May 1945 became VE (Victory in Europe) Day.

Despite crippling losses in the Pacific by late 1944 and early 1945 and the final threat to its home islands, Japan still showed no signs of surrender. The war in the Far East was only finally ended in August 1945 by the dropping of the atomic bomb, first on Hiroshima and then Nagasaki. The Japanese government surrendered on 14 August. The official surrender ceremony took place aboard the USS *Missouri* in Tokyo Bay on 2 September.

Lieutenant-Colonel Francis 'Gabby' Gabreski, 56th Fighter Group, 8th Air Force, who was the top-scoring USAAF 'ace' in Europe with twenty-eight victories.

USAF

ACKNOWLEDGEMENTS

I am grateful to the following people: Mike Bailey; Group Captain Antony Barwood OBE; Boeing Aircraft Co.; Tom Cushing; Douglas Aircraft; Don Downie; Ken Fields; Ken Godfrey; Larry Goldstein; Philip Jarrett; Jack Krause; Edward Leaf; Lockheed Corporation; Tom Lubbesmeyer, Boeing Co.; Merle Olmsted; Peter C. Smith; Elmer Vogel; Paul Wilson; Richard Ziegler, Boeing Co.

Fighters to the fore in the Second World War escorted the bombers, strafed and bombed targets and duelled on all fronts with enemy machines. These are R47D Thunderbolts of the 56th Fighter Group, 8th Fighter Command (including *Diablo*).

USAF

USA airpower in the Pacific in the Second World War contributed greatly to total victory. One of the most effective aircraft in this theatre was the heavily armed North American B-25 Mitchell which was used both as a bomber and 'strafer'. This B-25D version with its nose transparency painted over, from the 41st Bomb Group based on Tarawa in the Central Pacific, early in 1944, is making a low-level attack on Wotje Atoll in the Marshalls. The 41st returned to Hawaii in October 1944 for training with rockets and new B-25s. The B-25H first entered service in the Pacific in February 1944, armed with fourteen .50-inch Browning machine-guns, a nose-firing 75-mm cannon, and eight .5-inch rockets for anti-shipping strikes and ground-attack duties. It could also carry 3,000 lb of bombs.

USAF

After the First World War American aircraft companies like Boeing continued in business mainly by modernizing existing military biplanes. In 1920 Boeing rebuilt 111 wooden de Havilland 1916-design DH4 'Liberty Planes' as DH-4B. Between 1923 and 1925 183 of the British two-seat day bombers were rebuilt with Boeing-designed steel-tube fuselages as DH-4M-1 (M for Modernized). Thirty of these were delivered to the US Marine Corps under the naval designation O2B-1, one went to the US Post Office and six were delivered to Cuba.

Boeing

In 1923 the Dayton-Wright Company became part of Consolidated Aircraft Corporation of Buffalo, New York. The first trainer of Consolidated design was the PT-1, and 171 examples were produced for the AAC. The next significant model was the PT-3, seen here, of which 130 production examples were built. These were followed by 120 PT-3As.

via Philip Jarrett

One of the hardest battles for single-seat pursuit biplane supremacy in the 1920s was fought between Boeing and Curtiss. Ultimately, the mighty Seattle-based company ended the long run of Curtiss Hawk designs but the Garden City, New Jersey, company did not go down without strong resistance, and it produced a range of Hawk biplanes. The P-3 was the first radial-engined Hawk and was created by converting the last of the inline engined P-1As to take an uncowled 410hp Pratt & Whitney R-1340-9. In 1928 Curtiss received a contract for five P-3A examples (28-189/193).

via Philip Jarrett

P-3A 28-189 was flown with experimental ring cowlings and redesignated as the second XP-3A. It was later redesignated XP-21 when used to test fly the 300 hp R-985-1 Wasp Junior radial engine. Finally, 28-189 became a P-1F when fitted with the Curtiss V-1150-3 in-line engine.

via Philip Jarrett

The first aircraft to carry the P-6 designation was one of the five P-2 Hawks modified to race for the Air Corps in the 1927 US National Air Races. The XP-6A (P-1A 26-295) was placed first in the race at 201mph. On 19 October 1928 eighteen P-6 Hawks were ordered and deliveries began in 1929. The first ten P-6s had water-cooling for their V-1570-17, later known as the Conqueror, but the final eight P-6As had V-1570-23s cooled by ethylene glycol (commercially sold as Prestone). The P-6/-6A Hawks were followed by forty-six P-6Es, ordered on 8 July 1931 and delivered by the end of 1932. Seventy-one AT-4/-5/-5A advanced trainers delivered to the Army in 1927 were converted to pursuits in 1929.

via Philip Jarrett

Until 1924 the Army relied almost solely on the DH-4B and DDH-4M for its observation and light bombing requirements. By 1 December 1924 the Army had begun flight trials on no less than eleven two-seat biplanes powered by the tried and tested Liberty engine. The Douglas XO-2 was declared the winner and an order for seventy-five aircraft, the largest Army two-seat contract since 1918, was received on 16 February 1925. Douglas biplanes went on to become one of the longest-lived designs between the two world wars. Production deliveries of the first forty-five Douglas O-2s began in January 1926. O-2H is seen here, the most widely used model, with 141 examples delivered, between 1927 and 1929, to the Air Corps and National Guard.

via Philip Jarrett

Martin MB-2 64195, one of five night bombers ordered from Glenn Martin in 1920. This aircraft was a direct development of the MB-1 of 1918, with non-staggered wings hinged at the rear spars just outboard of the Liberty 12 piston engines for folding aft, much in the same manner as the British Handley-Page 0-400. The MB-2 was supplemented by fifteen NBS-1 Night Bomber Short Range types, the majority of which were built by Lowe, Willard and Fowler (LWF), Aeromarine and Curtiss. Although the MB-2s and NBS-1s never saw action, they are famous as the aircraft used to sink the ex-German First World War battleship *Ostfriesland* in the Billy Mitchell exercises of July 1921. The NBS-1s, the only production bombers designated as night bombers by the USAAC, were superceded by Keystone LB-5s and O6s in 1927/8.

Martin

Although the Curtiss XO-1 was among the unsuccessful contenders in the 1924 observation evaluation, it was re-engined with a Packard IA-1500 and proved successful in trials the following year. O-1 Falcon production models were powered by the 435hp Curtiss V-1150 (D-12) engine. Pictured is the O-1E version; thirty-seven were built, which made it the most numerous version.

via Philip Jarrett

Huff-Daland's single-engined XLB-1 (light-bomber) appeared in August 1925. A year later, in October 1926, the company produced the enlarged and heavier XHB-1, but it was still single-engined despite the Army board declaring earlier that year that two-engined machines were more satisfactory for bombardment operation. To replace the Army's ageing Martin NBS-1s, Huff-Daland bowed to Army requirements and in November 1926 produced a two-engined version, the XLB-5. Known as the 'Pirate', the new bomber was powered by war-surplus 400hp Liberty V engines. In March 1927 Huff-Daland became the Keystone Aircraft Corporation. Ten LB-5s with triple rudders (pictured) were delivered between July and December 1927, and twenty-five LB-5As, with twin rudders, were delivered between January and July 1928.

via Philip Jarrett

Between 1927 and 1932 210 Keystone bombers of nineteen different types were supplied to the Army Air Corps, mainly because they were cheap to purchase and economical to operate. Pictured is a Keystone B-6A (ex LB-10), which formed part of the last Army biplane bomber contract, for twenty-five Hornet-powered B-4A and thirty-nine Cyclone powered B-6A Keystones. (The separate designation for light and heavy bombers was discarded in 1930.) The B-6As were delivered between August 1931 and January 1932, and the B-4As between January and April 1932. By June 1932 Keystone bombers equipped no less than eleven Air Corps bombardment squadrons, while the training squadron at Kelly Field had a handful of B-5As and LB-7s.

via Philip Jarrett

Women workers stitching the upper wing fabric of a Thomas-Morse MB-3A single-seat pursuit. Asked by the Army to develop a single-seat fighter superior to the French Spad, Thomas-Morse had built four MB-3 prototypes, the first flying in the spring of 1919, and had followed this with fifty service models. In 1920 Boeing was a low bidder among 6 manufacturers competing for an Army contract for 200 improved Thomas-Morse MB-3A pursuits. This was the first sizeable order for new aircraft placed by the military since the Armistice and it provided the company with design experience that saw Boeing become the leading American supplier of single-seat pursuit aircraft between 1924 and 1936.

Boeing

The Thomas-Morse MB-3As differed from the MB-3 principally in having a revised cooling system, with radiators on each side of the fuselage by the cockpit instead of in the upper wing. After an Army pilot pulled the wings off an MB-3A and escaped with his life by baling out at low level near the Boeing factory, the company made minor structural changes and designed and built all new tail surfaces for the last fifty production models. Boeing abandoned the traditional wooden fuselage construction, which gradually gave way to the arc-welded steel-tube fuselage introduced in the Boeing PW-9 and the DH-4M. Thomas-Morse was absorbed by Consolidated Aircraft in August 1929.

Boeing

Opposite, above: An MB-3 model provided by Thomas-Morse as a sample flipped on to its back during a landing at a military airfield near Seattle, Washington, and so the first of the Boeing-built MB-3As was taken by road to a more suitable field at Camp Lewis, 50 miles south of Seattle. The flight was safely completed on 7 June 1922 but the Army test pilot failed to spot a ditch and this aircraft also ended up on its back!

Boeing

Below: Ten unique, armoured GA-1 ground-attack triplanes powered by two 435hp Liberty 12A engines were built by Boeing under an early postwar policy whereby the Army designed aeroplanes to its own requirements and then contracted their manufacture by the aviation industry under competitive bidding. Although not a Boeing design, the overweight and unpopular (with cadets) GA-1, which first flew in May 1921, was designated the Model 10.

Boeing

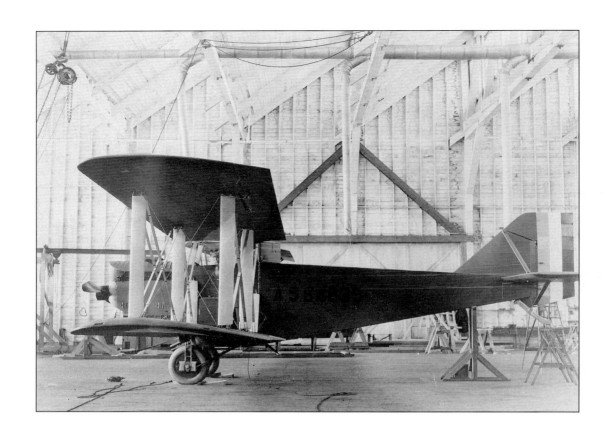

A USA Army Air Service Consolidated PT-1 two-seat training plane with an 180hp water-cooled Hispano Suiza eight-cylinder engine over Bowman Field, Louisville, Kentucky, April 1928. The pilot, in the front seat, is 2nd Lieutenant John Russ and Private Chester Lamppin is in the rear seat under the top wing. Both were members of the USA Army's 465th Pursuit Squadron, US Army Air Service Reserve. However, this squadron did not have any pursuit aircraft, just one de Havilland and several PT-1s. Captain Sidney Park and Private Glenn Smith, both members of the 465th, flying in a civilian Lincoln Standard, took this photograph.

via Ken Godfrey

Opposite, above: Two GA-2 biplane prototypes powered by an untried single 750hp Engineering Division W-18 engine were built by Boeing. Since the new engine was unavailable at the time of the contract, a wooden mock-up was delivered!

Boeing

Below: In August 1923 the Army Air Service ordered five DT-2s from the Navy production run for use as Douglas World Cruisers, with interchangeable wheel and float landing gears, for the first round-the-world flight. On 17 March 1924 four of the DWCs left Clover Field at Santa Monica, California, and headed for Alaska. Two of the DWCs were lost but *Chicago* (seen here), flown by Captain Lowell H. Smith and Lieutenant Leslie P. Arnold, and *New Orleans* piloted the 27,534 mile journey in 175 days, which included 15 days, 11 hours and 7 minutes of actual flying time, arriving at Seattle on 28 September. In 1924 the USA Army Air Service/Air Corps began ordering derivatives of the Cloudster as O-2 Corps observation aircraft. By 1926 Douglas had delivered no less than 885 of these observation biplanes in more than 50 versions, of which 246 machines were for the USA Army Air Service/Air Corps).

Douglas

In October 1925 Boeing was awarded a contract for twenty-five improved PW-9As and in June 1926 fifteen were ordered as PW-9B, but these (26-443/457) were converted to PW-9C before completion; PW-9C 26-443 is seen here. In August 1926 a second batch of twenty-five PW-9Cs was ordered. An order for 16 PW-9Ds in August 1927 brought total PW-9 production to 123.

Boeing

Opposite, above: Production experience with the MB-3As and careful study of the newest aerodynamic and structural concepts convinced Boeing engineers that they could produce a better pursuit plane than anything then available. The main source of dissatisfaction with the MBH-3A was the wooden fuselage. Welded steel tubing had been used successfully during the First World War. The gas welding process with hand torches had disadvantages, so Boeing developed an arc welding process. The new fuselage construction was so successful that the Army gave Boeing additional DH-4 modification contracts that called for replacement of the original wooden fuselages with steel ones. Financed as a private company venture, the first Boeing pursuit, the Model 15 (XPW-9 Experimental Pursuit, Watercooled Design No. 9), flew on 29 April 1923. It was powered by a 435hp Curtiss D-12 engine. By 16 December 1924 Boeing had received production orders for thirty PW-9s (25-295/324). PW-9 25-301 is seen here.

Boeing

Below: P-12 29-353 *Pan American*, the first Army Model 102 built, was turned over to Captain Ira C. Eaker on 26 February 1929, shortly after his famous 150-hour endurance flight, 1–7 January 1929, over Los Angeles, California, where air-to-air refuelling was successfully employed.

Boeing

In 1929 ninety examples of the Model 102B (P-12B) (29-333 is seen here) were ordered, the largest single Army order for fighters since 1921. The optional 55-gallon auxiliary fuel tank is fitted under the belly.

Boeing

AAC 29-329, the first P-12B, was modified by the AAC as XP-12G to test turbo-superchargers and ring cowlings, and fitted with a three-bladed prop to absorb the additional power, before reverting to P-12B.

Boeing

From June to September 1930 eight Loening OA-2 amphibians were built at Bristol, Pennsylvania, by Keystone, which had bought Grover Loening's company. The experimental Wright Tornado inverted, air-cooled engine proved so disastrous (it took almost an hour for the aircraft to climb to 10,000 ft!) that the engine was never again used by the Army.

via Philip Jarrett

Between 1928 and 1931 the Thomas-Morse Company won orders for 177 Pratt & Whitney Wasp-powered O-19 observation biplanes. Of these seventy-one, ordered on 12 June 1930, were O-19Cs, which began appearing in November 1930 with a Townend drag ring cowl and tail wheel. O-19 series aircraft served with eight of the thirteen Army observation squadrons at home and overseas in 1931.

via Philip Jarrett

The thirty-third P-12D (31-273) was redesignated XP-12H when the AAC fitted it with an experimental geared Pratt & Whitney GISR-1340E engine. However, this proved to be unsatisfactory and the plane was reconverted to a P-12D in June 1932.

Boeing

Opposite, above: The Detroit-Lockheed XP-900 (YP-24) of 1931 was Lockheed's first fighter, a joint effort of the erstwhile Detroit Aircraft Company and Lockheed. The two-seat aircraft became a casualty of the 1929 Depression and a thirteen-plane contract was cancelled by the AAC in 1931. The XP-900 had a metal fuselage constructed in Detroit and was shipped to Burbank for final assembly with a California-made plywood wing.

Lockheed

Below: The Model 227 (P-12D, XP-12H) resulted from slightly modifying the last 35 of the original 131 aircraft P-12C order. Deliveries began on 25 February 1931 and finished on 28 April.

Boeing

On 3 March 1931 the AAC
ordered 135 P-12Es (Model
234); 32-44 is seen here. The
enlarged 'Panama' headrest
contains a life raft. Some
586 aircraft in the P-12/F-4B
series were delivered to the
Army and the Navy (and a
few overseas), the last on
28 February 1933.

Boeing

P-12E (Model 234) 32-47 in AAC livery, 29 May 1934.

Boeing

Opposite, above: The last twenty-five P-12Es were completed as P-12Fs (Model 251), while 3242, seen here, became the P-12J when it was used at Wright Field to test a supercharged Pratt & Whitney SR-134OH engine and a special bomb sight. It became a YP-12K to test the SR-134OE fuel-injected engine, before reverting to P-12E.

Boeing

Below: P-12F (32-101), 11 May 1932, six days before delivery. The twenty-fifth and last of the production run, it was fitted with an experimental enclosed cockpit canopy.

Boeing

The Model 214 (Y1B-9) was a military development that applied the aerodynamic and structural concepts of the Monomail to bomber construction. Traditionally, bombers had, up until this point, been biplane types, mainly of all-wood construction. Both the Model 214 and 215 were developed at company expense. The Model 215 (XB-901, later YB-9) was powered by 600hp Pratt & Whitney Hornet engines. The first flew on 13 April 1931. The Model 214 (Y1B-9), originally powered by 600hp liquid-cooled Curtiss Conqueror engines, flew on 5 November 1931. A service test order for five improved Model 246s was placed in August 1931 under the Army designation Y1B-9A (seen here in flight with the XP-936) and the two prototypes were purchased at the same time. The new bomber raised the speed of bombers to 186mph, some 5mph above that of contemporary fighters, marking the beginning of a modern American bombardment force.

Boeing

The Curtiss XA-8 Shrike was designed to an AAC request for an all-metal low-wing attack monoplane and flew for the first time in June 1931. Modern features included wing slots and flaps to minimize landing speed, the first to appear on an American combat aircraft. The XA-8 proved better than its competitor, the Fokker XA-7, and on 29 September 1931 five service-test YA-8s and eight Y1A-8s, all powered by 600hp inline Prestone-cooled Curtiss Conqueror V-1570-31 engines, were ordered. One of the YA-8s was later re-engined with an air-cooled 625hp Pratt & Whitney R-1620-9 Hornet radial engine. This proved far superior to the liquid-cooled Conqueror, and was redesignated A-10.

via Philip Jarrett

A Curtiss A-12 Shrike, one of forty-six production models ordered on 27 February 1933. Following the successful installation of the Pratt & Whitney Hornet radial, all A-12s, which were delivered to the 3rd Attack Group at Fort Crockett, Texas, between November 1933 and February 1934, were powered by the 670hp Wright R-1820-21 Cyclone radial engine. Also, the A-12 differed from the previous A-8 and A-10 designs in having a rear gun installation just behind the pilot to house the rear gunner and a .30-in machine-gun. Four .30-in guns were again located in pairs in the landing gear fairings and four 100-lb or ten 30-lb bombs could be carried under the wings. In 1935 the A-8s and an A-12 were allocated to the new 37th Attack Squadron at Langley Field.

via Philip Jarrett

A Curtiss A-12 Shrike with skis, 13 February 1936. In 1936, when the 3rd Attack Group received Northrop A-17s, fifteen A-12s were sent to Kelly Field, Texas, for use as trainers, while twenty went to the 26th Attack Squadron in Hawaii, where they served until 1941.

via Philip Jarrett

Boeing's Model 248, which first flew on 20 March 1932, was the first all-metal monoplane fighter. Boeing built three XP-936 prototypes at its own expense, but the Army loaned Pratt & Whitney 522hp SR-1340E Wasp engines, instruments and military equipment for the project, which was carefully co-ordinated with the Army to ensure that its requirements were met. Pictured is the third XP-936, which went to Selfridge Field, Michigan, where it was tested by the Army. During service tests the XP-26s became Y1P-26 and finally simply P-26. After testing, on 15 June 1932, the Army purchased the XP-936s as XP-26.

Boeing

Opposite, above: The Glenn Martin Co. had a very successful partnership with the USA Army in the 1920s and was determined to be among the main suppliers of the next generation of all-metal, twin-engined monoplane bombers and Martin's Model 123 was developed as a private venture. Unlike the Boeing B-9 the Martin Model had an internal bomb bay and was the first American bomber to have a front gun turret fitted. The prototype Model 123 was delivered to the USA Army on 20 March 1932 and designated XB-907 for trials at Wright Field. An official order for forty-eight aircraft was issued on 17 January 1933. Deliveries of the first production Martin 139 models started in June 1934. This version had two enclosed cockpits for the pilot and radio-operator/rear gunner. In 1931 the US AAC was charged with coastal defence and several YB-10s and B-12s were fitted with floats for operation on water. A total of 109 B-10Bs, the last in 1942, followed before the type was replaced by the B-17 and B-18.

via Philip Jarrett

Below: P-26A, 16 December 1933. The 'Peashooter' was the first all-metal monoplane in Air Corps pursuit-squadron service and 111 P-26As were ordered by the AAC. Top speed was 222mph, 27mph faster than the P-12F, but fell 800 ft short (30,700 ft) of the biplane's absolute ceiling. Two P-26Bs were followed by twenty-three P-26Cs, all remodelled as P-26B while in service. All production P-26s – 136 were delivered between 1933 and 1936 – were modified by the additiion of wing flaps to reduce the high landing speeds to that of the contemporary biplanes.

Boeing

X13372, the Model 299, seen here at its roll out at Boeing Field, Seattle, 17 July 1935, when, because its wingspan was greater than the width of the hangar door, it had to be rolled out sideways on wheeled dollies. The Model 299 was flown for the first time on 28 July by the company test pilot Leslie Tower. The clean lines of the Model 299 owed much to the sleek Model 247 airliner, which was scaled up into the much bigger Model 299 by using many of the engineering innovations that had been developed on the earlier Model 294 (XB-15) project.

Boeing

Opposite, above: When on 14 April 1934 the Army General Staff issued a request for design proposals for 'Project A', an aircraft capable of carrying a 1-ton bomb 5,000 miles to hit targets in Hawaii or Alaska, Boeing proposed the Model 294 (XBLR-1 long-range experimental bomber). On 28 June 1934 Boeing were awarded a contract for design data, wind-tunnel tests and a mock-up. The massive four-engined bomber took three years to build, weighed over 35 tons, was almost 88 ft long and had a 149-ft span with passageways built inside the wing to enable the crew to make minor repairs to the four Pratt & Whitney R-1830-11 engines while the aircraft was in flight. Armed with six machine-guns, it contained complete living and sleeping quarters with sound-proofed, heated and ventilated cabins. It was at that time the largest aircraft in the world. Redesignated XB-15 before its first flight on 15 October 1937, the XB-15 joined the 2nd Bomb Group (BG) in August 1938 and set a number of records.

Boeing

Below: The USAAC continued the development of the low-level attack aircraft as their mainstay support aircraft during the 1930s. In 1934 Curtiss submitted its Model 76 to the Army as XA-14 in response to a requirement for a new two-seat twin-engine attack design. The XA-14, the first of that company's twin-engined aircraft, was tested at Wright Field with experimental Curtiss XR-1510 twin-row engines, and was then purchased by the Army. It was redelivered in standard Army marking (36-146) with 735hp Curtiss R-1670-5 engines. In 1936 thirteen service-test Y1A-18s were ordered and were virtually identical except for installation of 600hp Wright Cyclone engines.

via Peter C. Smith

The Model 299 signalled the beginning of the long line of famous Flying Fortress models used by the USAAF in the Second World War.

Boeing

Testing was almost complete and the Air Corps about to confer the title XB-17 on the Model 299, when, on 30 October 1935, the aircraft crashed with Major Ployer P. 'Pete' Hill (chief of Wright Field's Flight Testing Section) at the controls. Hill died later that day and Leslie Tower, Boeing test pilot, died a few days later. The subsequent investigation concluded that the crash was a result of the mechanical ground locks not having been unlocked prior to take-off.

Boeing

Also in 1935 Douglas began work at Santa Monica, California, on a massive, heavily armed, thirteen-gun, four-engined heavy bomber, originally called the XBLR-2, and capable of carrying a 37,100-lb bomb load. As the XB-19 (38-471) it first flew on 27 June 1941, but the type did not enter production and 38-471 was used during the Second World War as a transport.

Douglas

A North American BT-9 basic trainer on a night-instruction exercise. The BT-9 was adopted late in 1935 as a standard Army basic trainer and the first order was for forty-two examples. A second order for forty BT-9As with a fixed forward firing gun and a recording camera followed. In 1937 the Army ordered 117 BT-9Bs and production finished with 67 BT-9Cs for the Organized Reserve.

USAF

Ill-luck dogged the Y1B-17 service-test machine development. 36-149, the first Y1B-17, was rolled out on 30 September 1936, and it flew for the first time on 2 December, but on the 7th it nosed over during landing. However, the thirteen service test Y1B-17s went into service with the 2nd Bomb Group at Langley Field, Virginia, between March and August 1937, and were flown 1,800,000 miles over land and sea without a problem. Six of the Y1B-17s of the 2nd BG made the goodwill flight to Buenos Aires Argentina, in total 12,000 miles, without serious incident. The Fortress' place in history was assured.

Boeing

Northrop A-17 Attack aircraft in formation in the USA, mid-1930s. Delivery of 110 A-17s powered by the 750hp Pratt & Whitney R-1535-11 radial engine and armed with four fixed forward-firing .30-in guns in the wings began in August 1935. During 1936 these aircraft became standard equipment in USAAC attack units, such as the 3rd and 17th Attack Groups. The A-17 was followed by the A-17A, which had a more powerful 825hp Pratt & Whitney engine and retractable undercarriage.
Douglas

North American O-47 observation monoplanes over a city in the USA, late 1930s. The O-47 was a break from the tradition of the large, heavy two-seat observation aircraft that had been standard since 1915. It carried a crew of three, a pilot and observer in tandem in the cockpit and an observer/photographer in a deep-belly station clear of the wing. In 1937 164 O-47As with the 975hp Wright R-1820-49 piston radial were built at Inglewood, California, all in natural aluminium finish. These were followed by seventy-four O-47Bs powered by the more powerful 1,060hp Wright radial. The O-47 did not see service in the Second World War, having been replaced in the PR role by bombers and camera-carrying fighter conversions.

North American

Opposite, above: Originally designed in 1937 as a high-altitude interceptor, the P-38 was already in mass production before the outbreak of hostilities. Lockhead Burbank turned out 9,924 P-38 (Model 22) Lightnings. This is the first, the XP-38-LO 37-457, seen at March Field, California, which won Design Competition X-608 in February 1937. The XP-38 flew for the first time on 27 January 1939 at March Field, and was written off in a crash on 11 February 1939.

Lockheed

Below: The P-38 Lightning was one of the most easily recognizable fighters of the Second World War and together with the P-47 and P-51 formed the mainstay of the American fighter force in the USAAF between 1941 and 1945. Production contracts had been placed before the first YP-38 made its maiden flight on 16 September 1940, and the first deliveries of the P-38D Lightning to the USAAC followed in August 1941. Beginning in late 1941 a few Lightning I versions with unsupercharged Allisons were supplied to the RAF but the majority were diverted to the USAAF after Pearl Harbor.

via Philip Jarrett

Following the success of its Electra, in 1936 Lockheed brought out a similar but smaller plane identified as the Model 12. This was the fastest airplane of its size and type ever constructed in the USA, and was intended for the executive, corporation, feeder airline and sportsman pilot use. The ship carried six passengers, pilot and co-pilot. The XC-35 (c/n3501) was the first aircraft with a pressurized cabin to fly in the substratosphere, which it did on 7 May 1937. A modified Electra, it had a nearly spherical fuselage reinforced internally. The AAC received the Collier Trophy in 1937 for its high-altitude flights in the XC-35, which pioneered later military and civil developments in pressurized flight.

Lockheed

Development of the Model 75 monoplane by the Curtiss Airplane Division of the Curtiss-Wright Corporation, Buffalo, New York, began in November 1934. The AAC held a series of design competitions in 1935–6 between the Seversky P-35 and the Model 75. These were the first single-seat monoplane pursuits to feature a retractable undercarriage, enclosed cockpit and other modern features. In July 1936 production orders were placed for the Seversky pursuit and just three Y1P-36 service test models. However, on 7 July 1937 210 P-36 production models were ordered. The first of 178 P-36A, seen here, and 31 P-36C production models were delivered to the AAC in April 1938 (the other aircraft became the XP-40, which led to the P-40 series).

via Philip Jarrett

Curtiss P-36C Hawks in 1939 war-games livery. On 7 December 1941 four P-36As of the Hawaii-based 46th Pursuit Squadron shot down two Japanese bombers during the second phase of the attack on Pearl Harbor.

USAF

Boeing ceased work on the Model 300 transport in 1934 when priority was given to the Model 299 bomber. However, development was revived three years later in the Model 307, and utilized the wings, nacelles, engines and original tail surfaces, which were standard B-17 components married to an entirely new fuselage. All five of the TWA SA-307B Stratoliners of 1939–40 (42-88623/88627) were commandeered for use by Air Transport Command in 1942. They were flown by TWA crews mainly on the North and South Atlantic routes. The distinctive dorsal fin developed on this model was later used on the B-17E.

Boeing

In 1937 Alexander Kartveli's redesigned AP-1 monoplane pursuit was submitted to the AAC and it won for the Seversky company a production contract for seventy-seven P-35 aircraft. Armament comprised one .50-in and .30-in machine-gun in the engine cowling. Power was provided by a 1,050hp Pratt & Whitney R-1830-9 two-row radial. The last aircraft on the P-35 contract was completed as the XP-41 and it became the prototype for the Republic P-43 Lancer. P-35s of the 1st Pursuit Group are seen here in 1938.

USAF

Boeing PT-13As on the line at the USAAC Training Centre at Randolph Field, San Antonio, Texas, – 'the West Point of the Air' – January 1938. The Stearman Aircraft Co. of Wichita, Kansas, had been a Boeing subsidiary since 1934 and had made a name for itself with the production of Model 70/76 biplane trainers for the military. (The Model 75 had been in production for the Army since 1936.)

Boeing

PT-13A aerobating over Randolph Field, 15 January 1938. Three separate orders for ninety-two A75 (PT-13A) aircraft fitted with 220hp Lycoming R-680-7 radials, improved instrumentation, landing light, blind-flying hoods and electrical systems were ordered for Army service and these were delivered between April 1937 and June 1938. Altogether, 3,769 A75N1s would be built, including 2,942 for the AAC. The first Stearman came off the production line at Wichita in February 1945. All told, some 8,585 Model 70/76 Stearmans were built between 1933 and 1945.

Boeing

Between 1924 and 1936 Douglas delivered 885 observation biplanes in more than 50 versions, including 770 machines for the American services, 246 of which went to the Army Air Service and Army Air Corps. This is an O-46A, the last of the all-metal YO-31/Y10-43, O-43A, O-46A series of Douglas observation monoplanes, of which ninety were delivered between May 1936 and April 1937. Power was provided by a 725hp twin-row Pratt & Whitney R-1535-7 engine.

via Philip Jarrett

The Douglas B-18 Bolo was derived from the DC-2 transport and a contract for 133 Bolos was issued in January 1936 after the prototype DB-1 (Douglas Bomber 1) won a USAAC competition in August 1935 to replace the Martin B-10. A further 177 Bolos were ordered in June 1937. The type was finally replaced in service by the B-17 in 1942.

Douglas

A USAAC mechanic working on a
9th Bombardment Group B-18 Bolo at
Mitchel Field AAB, Long Island, New
York, 1938. In the background is a Douglas
O-46A of the 97th Observation Squadron.
via Larry Goldstein

A USAAC mechanic examines the wheel of a 9th Bombardment Group B-18 Bolo at Mitchel Field
AAB, Long Island, New York, 1938.

via Larry Goldstein

Boeing Y1B-17A 37-369, 30 January 1939. It was originally intended for completion as a static test aircraft but was subsequently redesignated Y1B-17A and used to test supercharged R-1820-51 engines.

Boeing

Opposite, above: An engine mechanic works on a A-17 motor at Mitchel Field, 1938.

via Larry Goldstein

Below: Another mechanic works on a Pratt & Whitney R-1535-7 radial of a Douglas O-46A of the 97th Observation Squadron at Mitchel Field, 1938.

via Larry Goldstein

The hoped for large production contracts for the B-17B (Model 299E, later Model 299M) were slow in coming. A requirement for ten B-17Bs had been received on 3 August 1937, but by 30 June 1938 orders stood at just thirty-nine. Problems with the superchargers, which tended to fail regularly, meant that the first B-17B (38–211) did not fly until 27 June 1939. The first B-17Bs were delivered to the AAC between October 1939 and 30 March 1940. During 1940 and 1941 many B-17Bs were revamped and fitted with new devices such as flush-type waist windows for .50-calibre guns.

Boeing

B-17D at Seattle, 5 February 1941. The forty-two B-17Cs ordered on 17 April 1940 required so many modifications, mostly due to combat experience in Europe by the RAF, that, on 9 September 1940, they were redesignated as B-17Ds. Extra armour plate was added and armament doubled in the ventral 'bathtub' and upper positions, while additional sockets were added for the .30-calibre nose gun, making seven guns in all. Self-sealing fuel tanks were installed and the bomb-release system was redesigned.

Boeing

In the late 1930s the AAC wanted a mass-produced, medium-altitude pursuit with two .30-calibre machine-guns. The Curtiss XP-40 with its liquid-cooled Allison V1710-19 could operate comfortably at 10,000 ft, and was faster and less expensive than the P-35. The XP-40 made its first flight on 14 October and at the AAC Pursuit Competition at Wright Field in May 1939 the XP-40 relegated the other pursuits to also-rans. An order received for 524 P-40s (later reduced to 200) was the largest yet placed for an American fighter. By the outbreak of war the P-40 was available in large numbers with highly trained pilots to fly them.

via Philip Jarrett

When the USAAC contracted the Bell Aircraft Corporation of Buffalo, New York, to build a single XP-39 prototype on 7 October 1937 it was the first tricycle, single-engined fighter to be ordered by that body. The XP-39 was a high-altitude pursuit interceptor, designed to operate at 15,000 ft and fire a nose-mounted 37-mm T-9 cannon built by the American Armament Corporation through the aircrew hub. The cannon mounting dictated the engine position, buried in the fuselage section aft of the cockpit. This in turn dictated the tricycle and undercarriage arrangement; the Allison V-1710 engine being the centre of gravity. A 10-ft extension drive shaft went to the reduction gearbox behind the propeller, and the radiators were mounted on each side of the fuselage just aft of the cockpit. The XP-39 prototype, seen here, flew on 6 April 1939. Twelve supercharged YP-39s and one unsupercharged YP-39A were ordered for evaluation and the P-39 Airacobra went into full production in August 1939.

Bell

In 1939 the USAAC ordered 143 A-20As and these were delivered to light bombardment groups in the USA and Hawaii. A simultaneous order for sixty-three A-20s to be fitted with R-2600-7 turbo-supercharged engines was not proceeded with and all except one (which became the XP-70 night-fighter protoype) were used as photo-reconnaissance aircraft. Two P-70 night-fighters equipped with airborne interception radar and ventral gun tray are seen here.

Douglas

Late in 1940 the USAAC ordered a small batch of Cessna T-50s for evaluation for advanced multi-engine pilot training and an order for thirty-three AT-8s followed.

Cessna

Opposite, above: The B-23 Dragon, seen here on 23 May 1941, was an improved B-18 with a redesigned fuselage and, for the first time in an American bomber, included a tail-gun position. A total of thirty-eight B-23s was ordered and the first of these flew on 27 July 1939. Most were used for a brief interlude on Pacific coastal patrol before being relegated to the training and transport roles.

via Philip Jarrett

Below: Contracts were awarded to Beech in 1940 for variants of the Model B-18S commercial light transport. In 1941 the AT-7 was ordered as a version of the C-45, seen here, and was used as a multi-engine transition and navigation trainer. Eventually, 1,141 A-7s in 4 models were built.

Beechcraft

In 1941 the Army Air Force followed its 1940 order for Cessna AT-8s with a further contract for more Cessna twin-engined trainers. The power plants were changed from 295hp Lycomings to 245hp Jacobs R-775-9s, and the new designation AT-17 was applied.

Cessna

Opposite, above: The AT-11 Kansan was evolved from the AT-7 in 1941 for bombing and gunnery training. The USAAF received 1,582 examples, including 36 modified as AT-11As for navigation training, as well as A24 AT-11s repossessed from an order destined for the Netherlands.

Cessna

Below: A total of 858 SBD-3 Dauntlesses was built, the first being delivered on 18 March 1941. This is SBD-3A (A-24A), one of seventy-eight with the deck hook removed, delivered from the USA Navy production line at El Segundo between June and October 1941 with 'USA Army' stencilled on the tail. In November 1941 fifty-two A-24As were shipped to the Philippines for use by the 27th Bomb Group (Light) but subsequent operational use in the Dutch East Indies and from Australia revealed that they lacked range, were too slow and were vulnerable to enemy fighters. A total of 763 A-24As (SBD-4 equivalent) and A-24Bs (SBD-5) was built.

Douglas

A contract for 250 Hudson bombers, a military development of the Lockheed Model 14 Super Electra, was placed by the British Purchasing Commission in June 1938 to meet a requirement for a coastal reconnaissance bomber. The Model B14L (Hudson Mk.I/N7205) flew on 10 December 1938 at Burbank. Ultimately, 1,500 aircraft were produced for RAF Coastal Command and the RAAF before the bomber was included in Lend-Lease procurement programmes and became designated A-28. Some 52 A-28s and 450 A-28As were allocated to the RAF from AAC stocks.

Lockheed

In the summer of 1940 Britain had placed an order for 188 Lockheed Ventura Mk.I bombers (plus a further 487 Mk.IIs). A B-34-VE is seen here. The Ventura was a Vega military development of the Lodestar airliner. A total of 200 Venturas, designated B-34, were serial numbered 41-38020/38219 for the USAAF but most of these were assigned to Britain under Lend-Lease in August 1941. The USAAF received 20 B-34-VEs upon the entry of the USA into the war, and later ordered 550 B-37-LO versions, but only 18 were ever built. In the Second World War Lockheed-Vega turned out 3,028 Ventura and Harpoon bomber versions of the prewar Lodestar 18. The biggest user of the Ventura was the RAF, which received 675 Mk.I and Mk.II versions, while the USA Navy operated the bulk of PV-1 and PV-2 Harpoons.

Lockheed

With a change of engine, the Model 414-56 was designated A-29. A total of 417 A-29s (41-23223/23638) was built, together with 384 A-29As with troop benches for optional transport use. A number of the 800 A-29/A-29As allocated to Britain (41-23325 is seen here) were repossessed, and, with the dorsal turret deleted, were used for USAAC bomber-crew training and for anti-submarine duties during 1942 and 1943 over the Atlantic.

via Philip Jarrett

In 1941 American bombing plans included 3,740 intercontinental Convair B-36 bombers, based in the USA, which would be capable of bombing targets in Europe. A specification issued on 11 April 1941 called for a very long-range bomber capable of 10,000 miles range without refuelling and able to carry a 10,000-lb bomb load at least half the distance. It also had to have a maximum speed of 400mph and an operational ceiling of 35,000 ft. In order to reach the original range specification it would have to carry 21,116 gallons of fuel in the wings. As if this was not enough, the sheer size of the aircraft would require a 5,000-ft runway – an almost impossible task at the time. Convair Fort Worth received a contract for 100 B-36 aircraft on 23 July 1943 after it appeared that B-36s would be needed to attack Japan, but the capture of the Mariana Islands allowed B-29s to be based there to attack the Japanese mainland and B-36 deliveries were no longer critical. Convair rolled out the first XB-36 (42-13570 is seen here) on 8 September 1945, and it first flew on 8 August 1946.

Convair

On 12 July 1940 Boeing was advised by the War Department that orders for 512 more B-17s would be raised, but shortages material delayed production of the B-17E and the example did not make its maiden flight until 5 September 1941, four months behind schedule. B-17E 41-2459 is seen here at Shallufa, Egypt, en route to join the 19th Bomb Group in Java accompanied by a second 'E', 41-2461. On 10 December 1941 the first AF mission of the Second World War was flown when five B-17s of the 19th BG flying from Clark Field attacked Japanese ships near Vigan in the Philippines. The 19th BG fought gallantly, but lost the battle in the Philippines after the Japanese invasion. 41-2459 and 41-2461 were first used in action on 16 January 1942. Lieutenant J.L. 'Duke' Du Frane's and Major C.F. Necrasson's crews respectively had to force land at Kendari, Borneo, and were strafed by Zeros. Du Frane's B-17 was disabled but his crew escaped and were later evacuated to Java. The aircraft was later blown up during the American retreat.

Group Captain Antony Barwood

Fresh from the Northrop factory, brand-new Vultee Vengeance dive-bombers are lined up on the airfield at Hawthorne, California, *c*. 1941. Northrop was one of two plants that produced the aircraft; the other was at Nashville. The V-72 Vengeance was among the new types ordered from the USA in 1940 by Great Britain. In March 1941 the USAAC also placed orders for the Vultee dive-bomber, then designated A-31. Deliveries began just as the USA was plunged into war and some of those models earmarked for Britain were repossessed.

via Peter C. Smith

A fine aerial view of EZ856 being flight-tested over the Californian foothills, *c*. 1941. Equipped to full AAC standards, the Vengeance was redesignated A-35A, with four .50-in machine-guns in the wings and a single .50-in gun in the rear cockpit. Of the 931 A-35A and -B versions built, only 369 were operated by the Army, many being re-assigned for target-towing duties. In Allied service, however, the Vengeance proved very successful, with the RAF in India and Burma and with the RAAF in New Guinea.

via Peter C. Smith

A flight of North American BT-14 basic trainers sweeps over the USAAC Training Centre at Randolph Field, San Antonio, Texas, 13 June 1941. At this time there were 350 of these low-wing monoplanes at Randolph, where student aviators learned to spread their wings before graduating and receiving commissions in the Air Corps Reserve.

USAF

The P-43 Lancer was Republic Aviation Corporation's first production combat aircraft, *c.* 1941. First flown in 1941, the P-43 was the world's first 300mph fighter and the first all-metal pursuit plane with semi-elliptical fuselage. A contract for fifty-four P-43s was placed in 1940 and this was followed by another order for eighty P-43A versions with a more powerful engine. Pictured is P-43A-1 41-31449, second of the last production run of 125. Some export versions of the Lancer were flown in combat by the Chinese Air Force against the Japanese. In 1942 most surviving USAAC P-43s were used in the reconnaissance role.

Republic

Opposite, above: Seversky P-35A 41-17435, one of 100 ordered originally as EP-106s for export to Sweden as the J9. Deliveries to the Flygvapnet began in 1939 but were suspended in mid-1940. On 24 October that year all sixty undelivered EP-106s were commandeered and redesignated P-35A. This model differed from the P-35 in having a more powerful 1,200hp R-1830-45 engine and one .30-in machine-gun in each wing. By the end of 1941 forty-eight P-35As had arrived in the Philippines; forty were quickly lost on the ground in the Japanese onslaught and the rest were destroyed in combat.

Republic

Below: The North American B-25 Mitchell was the result of an Air Corps requirement for a medium bomber in 1938. In September 1939 the AAC placed an order for 184 B-25s, including 40 B-25As and 120 B-25B variants. A total of 130 Mitchells was delivered at the time of the Japanese attack on Pearl Harbor, 7 December 1941. The 17th Bomb Group (Medium) at Pendleton, Oregon, was the first AAF group to use B-25s, and was at full strength with fifty-two Mitchells in September 1941. During an anti-shipping strike off the west coast of the USA on 24 December a 17th BG B-25A sank a Japanese submarine. Led by Lieutenant-Colonel James H. Doolittle, sixteen B-25B crews from the 17th BG were the only bombers ever to attack the enemy from an aircraft carrier, when on 18 April 1942 they took off from the USS *Hornet* and bombed Tokyo. B-25D 43-3374 is seen here, which North American Aviation restored for the tenth anniversary of the Doolittle raid and is repainted as 40-2344 to represent the B-24B that Doolittle flew. This aircraft is now on display at the USAF Museum at Dayton, Ohio.

North American

The first B-25C was flown on 9 November 1941 (41-12633 is seen here). B-25C production was completed in May 1943, with 1,619 examples built.

USAF

Lockheed P-38E 41-2082, one of 210 Es built, beginning in November 1941. The P-38F followed the E into production early in 1942 and 527 examples were built at Burbank. The first unit to operate the P-38 was the 342nd Composite Group operating from Icelandic bases. The first German aircraft shot down by a USAAF fighter occurred on 15 August 1942 when two P-38Fs from the 27th Squadron of the 1st Fighter Group and a P-40 destroyed a FW 200 Condor near Iceland. Beginning in November 1942 P-38s also saw large-scale service in North Africa and the Mediterranean theatre.

via Tom Cushing

While the P-40 operated extensively in most theatres during the Second World War, from the Alaskan wastes to low-level ground-attack operations with the Desert Air Force in North Africa, and in the far-flung Pacific campaign, the P-40's greatest claim to fame is undoubtedly due to the achievements of less than 100 aircraft of Major (later General) Claire Chennault's American Volunteer Group in China. More popularly known as the 'Flying Tigers', the AVG was formed in 1941 with three pursuit squadrons trained in Burma. Chennault (right) is seen here with Major-General Henry H. 'Hap' Arnold, Chief of the AAF.

USAF

When they went into combat on 20 December 1941, two weeks after Pearl Harbor, the 'Flying Tigers' shot down six Mitsubishi bombers. Operating in a hostile environment using equipment inferior to the enemy, the P-40s, each with their red and white shark-teeth emblems on the nose, created one of the most memorable of all P-40 legends. Before being disbanded in 1942, the AVG had shot down 286 Japanese aircraft for the loss of just 12 pilots. Chennault's AVG supplied experienced pilots as well as the name 'Flying Tigers' to the 23rd Fighter Group, which was activated in China on 4 July 1942. Using P-40s, and later P-51s, the 23rd provided air defence for the Chinese terminus of the 'Hump' route over the Himalayas from India and its operations extended beyond China to Burma, French Indochina and Formosa.

via Philip Jarrett

In 1931 Douglas Aircraft bought just over a half share in Jack Northrop's El Segundo operation south of Santa Monica and had set about recreating the company's A-17 (Model 8) attack-bomber design for the overseas export market. Douglas built 351 A-17-8As. In 1942, thirty-one 1,200hp R-1820-87-powered Douglas 8A-5s of a batch of thirty-six ordered for Norwegian use in Canada were requisitioned by the USAAC as A-33s. 42-13594 is seen here.

USAF

Douglas C-53 41-20092 being loaded at Miami, Florida for flight with miscellaneous cargo for Air Transport Command Base, 29 January 1942. Operated under contract by Pan American Airways, these planes of the DC-3 type were the backbone of ATC operations in this area. They took off from Miami Airport and followed the Caribbean to the north coast of South America, refuelling at ATC bases along the route.

USAF

North American AT-6A Harvards in formation from Napier Field, Dothan, Alabama, March 1942. North American developed the AT-6 from their original NA-16 design of 1935. Ever since it won the March 1937 Air Corps design competition to produce a new basic trainer, the company earned an enviable worldwide reputation for rugged, dependable training aircraft. In 1940 the designation changed from BC-1A to AT-6A. The Inglewood plant turned out 517 AT-6As and a second production line at Dallas, Texas, built 1,032 AT-6As and 2,970 AT-6Cs. Production of the AT-6D reached a staggering 4,388 examples and was followed by 956 AT-6F versions, most of which went to the USA Navy as the SNJ-6. Well in excess of 2,000 AT-6s remained in service with the USAAF after the Second World War.

via Philip Jarrett

B-17Es – the nearest is 41-2557 – on a training flight from Ephrata, Washington, 13 June 1942.

via Philip Jarrett

Opposite, above: Boeing B-17E 41-2435 of the 40th Bomb Squadron, 19th Bomb Group, seen here over the Owen Stanleys, was shot down off Buna on 12 August 1942. Note the power-operated Bendix belly gun turret, which was installed in the first 112 Es on the production line, and was fired by a gunner lying prone and facing aft, sighting the guns through a periscope arrangement of angled mirrors.

Ken Fields

Below: In the later 1930s the steady development of the single-engined AAC attack aircraft resulted in larger and larger aircraft being built to perform this role. In 1936 Douglas took the next step, upgrading the power plant to a twin-engined concept. On 2 October 1940 the AAC ordered 999 A-20B models, and deliveries to the AAF commenced in December 1941. The final Boston development was the A-20, seen here on 14 October 1942, fitted with Wright R-26000-7 Cyclone 14 engines. With American entry into the war, 162 Douglas-built and 194 Boeing-built models for the RAF were diverted to the AAF, where the type was universally known as the A-20 Havoc. These attack bombers had a solid 'gun nose' with awesome fire-power supplied by 20-mm cannon and .50-calibre machine-guns.

via Peter C Smith

On 29 May 1942 the first P-51 for USAAF service was flown. It differed from the Mustang I in having four 20-mm cannon in place of the six machine-guns used on the RAF version. In 1942 the first twenty P-51s were used as tactical reconnaissance aircraft equipped with two cameras. In 1943 they were used by the 68th Observation Group. In 1942 North American began fitting the 1,300hp Packard-built V-1650-3 Merlin to two XP-78 models, later redesignated XP-51B. Planners in the AAF saw the Mustang as a tactical fighter so the first deliveries of P-51Bs (43-7116 is seen here) in November 1943 were assigned to three groups of the tactical 9th Air Force at the expense of 8th Fighter Command, whose need for a long-range escort fighter was critical.

North American

Opposite, above: In 1942 the Cessna T-50 was adopted by the USAAF as a light personnel transport, designated C-78 (later UC-78) and named the Bobcat; UC-78 42-58125 is seen here. The USAAF received 1,297 Bobcats, as well as 17 T-50s commandeered for use as UC-78As.

Cessna

Below: The Mustang was designed originally to meet British requirements after North American Aviation at Inglewood, California, was approached by the British Purchasing Commission in April 1940 to produce the Curtiss H-87 (P-40D). North American's suggestion that they build a brand-new and infinitely superior fighter instead using the same 1,150hp Allison V-1710-39 engine was accepted and North American succeeded in delivering the NA-73X prototype in just 117 days. It was flown for the first time on 26 October 1940. The first Mustang I production NA-73 was flown on 23 April 1941. The first version ordered by the USAAF was the A-36A (NA-97), a ground-attack variant, which is seen here. The A-36A few in September 1942 and 500 were produced by March 1943. From October 1942 to March 1943 500 A-36A dive-bomber models fitted with 1,325hp liquid-cooled V-1710-87 engines, boosted for low-level operation, dive brakes and bomb racks were built. These served in Tunisia and India and proved so successful that fighter-bombers were used on close-support missions for the rest of the war.

North American

Before the Second World War Lockheed had been successful with their four-engined Model 49 airliner, for which the company had begun design studies in 1938. Pan American and TWA had showed initial interest and the Model 44 Excalibur, with accommodation for twenty-one passengers and a top speed of 241mph, evolved. This led, in 1939, to a bigger and faster design, the Model 49 Constellation. TWA and Pan American each ordered 40 Double Cyclone powered Constellations but with the outbreak of war production switched instead to 180 C-69 long-range transports for the USAAF. The first aircraft, NX25600 (43-10309 is seen here), was completed in December 1942 and first flew on 9 January 1943. Only 15 C-69s were delivered, but these were followed after the war by 233 civil airliner versions.

Lockheed

Needing suitable four-engined transport aircraft, early in 1942 the USAAC commandeered the DC-4A Santa Monica production line and the first thirty-four aircraft were designated C-54 Skymaster, one of which is seen here. No prototype was built, the first production aircraft (s/n 3050/41-20137) flying on 14 February 1942. During the Second World War the C-54s were operated in North Africa, over the 'Hump' from India to Alaska and to other battle fronts by Air Transport Command, which came into being in December 1942. A second production line was subsequently opened in Chicago and this and the Santa Monica plant between them turned out 207 C-54As. These were followed by 220 C-54D models, 75 Santa Monica-built C-54Es and 76 C-54Gs, to bring total C-54 production to 952.

via Philip Jarrett

B-24D Liberator *Virgin II* of the 90th BG taxi-ing out on to the runway at Jackson Drome near Port Moresby, New Guinea, 9 December 1942.

A waist gunner watching from the port hatch of a B-17 during a photo-reconnaissance mission over New Guinea, 1942.

C-47-DL Skytrain *Sad Sack* 41-1853, an early Long-Beach-built model, from a Southern Combat Air Transport unit with a top cover of Curtiss P-40s, somewhere in the south-west Pacific theatre, 1942. Named Skytrain by the USAAF, this was the first fully militarized version of the DST/DC-3 series, and 965 were delivered, beginning on 23 December 1941. The unarmed Douglas Transports of Southern Combat Air Transport flew regular schedules between New Zealand, Noumean, Efate, Espiritu Santo, Guadalcanal and, later, the Solomon chain.

Douglas

Opposite, above: B-17F-55-BO 42-29467, 18 December 1942. Named *Flak Dodger*, this aircraft flew in the Mediterranean theatre of operations, initially with the 348th Bomb Squadron, 99th Bomb Group, The 'F' looked similar to the B-17E, except for a frameless Plexiglas nose, but no less than 400 changes and modifications were made, most of them being carried out on the production line itself. In Italy B-17s equipped six bomb groups in the 5th Bomb Wing.

Boeing

Below: Field modifications to B-17E 41-2432 *The Last Straw* in the 63rd Bomb Squadron, 43rd Bomb Group, show an early attempt to improve the forward fire-power of the Fortress in the Pacific by installing tail guns in the nose.

USAF

In 1941 Northrop began forming a long-range flying-wing bomber and a development contract was placed with them by the USAAF early in 1942. Northrop built four 7,100-lb scale models and on 5 July 1942 the XB-35 mock-up was approved. The prototype XB-35 did not fly until 25 June 1946.

Northrop

Douglas A-20B-DL Havocs of the 97th Bomb Squadron, 47th Bomb Group (Light), 12th Air Force, in North Africa, c. 1942. The 47th BG, together with A-20Bs of the 68th Observation Group and those of the 15th Squadron, operated in North Africa from 1942. When the Axis forces broke through at Kassrine Pass in February 1943 the 47th, though undermanned and undersupplied, flew eleven missions on 22 February to attack advancing armoured columns and thus stop the enemy's offensive. For their actions, the 47th were awarded a DUC (Distinguished Unit Citation).

USAF

In July 1942, under the command of the 9th Air Force, the fifty-seven B-25Cs of the 12th Bombardment Group landed in Egypt after flying in from Florida via the Antilles, Brazil, Ascension Island and central Africa. The 'desert-pink' coloured bombers flew ninety-one missions and dropped over 1,500,000 lb of bombs.

USAF

The 12th Bomb Group made their first raid in support of British forces on 14 August 1942. Forty-six B-25s took part in the Battle of El Alamein, losing ten of their number, including four on one night raid. In August 1943 the 12th BG transferred to the 12th Air Force for raids on Sicily and Italy. In August 1944 the Group moved to the China, Burma and India theatre. After the Allied landings in North Africa in November 1942, three more B-25 groups, the 310th, 321st and 340th, joined the 12th Air Force in the Mediterranean theatre of operation.

USAF

XP-49 40-762 stratospheric research aircraft regularly flew above 40,000 ft. This P-38 (Model 522) first flew in November 1942 and was used for high-altitude research and pressure-cabin development.

Lockheed

A third wartime B-24 Liberator production line was brought into operation at the Douglas Tulsa plant in Oklahoma in March 1943. In total, 962 B-24s, including 582 B-24Hs and 205 B-24Js, were turned out there.

Douglas

Opposite, above: Jack Krause of the 15th Anti Submarine Squadron at Jacksonville, Florida, and Cuba, 1943. Like thousands of other 'non-coms', Jack was one of the unsung heroes of the Second World War air operations, who worked unceasingly on the aircraft in their care, day and night, in all climes and in all weathers. From early 1944 to the end of the war Jack Krause served in the 755th Bomb Squadron Armament Section of the 458th Bomb Group, 2nd Air Division, 8th Air Force, at Horsham St Faith, near Norwich, England. Each group in every theatre would never have functioned properly without its ground crews. 'Ground-pounders' also included the ordnancemen, sub-depot personnel, medical orderlies, fire fighters, quartermasters and administrators.

Jack Krause collection

Below: A Douglas C-47, one of many engaged in bringing up supplies and equipment for the Allied forces, comes in to land at a north African air base held by American troops, 1943.

USAF

The Martin Marauder was designed to a specification issued by the Air Corps on 25 January 1939 for a new high-speed medium bomber. In September 1939 the USAAF ordered 201 aircraft without the benefit of prototypes but accidents during early test and training flights earned the aircraft an unwelcome reputation as a 'widow-maker'. On 8 December 1941, the day after Pearl Harbor, fifty-three of the first fifty-six B-26As of the 22nd Bomb Group took off from Langley Field, Virginia, for Australia. In April 1942 they saw action for the first time, during attacks on New Guinea. During 1942 B-26As saw wide-ranging service, being employed as torpedo bombers in the Battle of Midway in June and, based in Alaska, for long-range strikes on the Aleutian Islands.

Martin

Opposite, above: A-20B-DL Havocs of the 47th Bomb Group (Light), 12th Air Force, over Tunisia, early 1943. This group remained on combat status during March and April 1943 while training for medium-level bombardment.

USAF

Below: The 47th Bomb Group took part in the reduction of Pantelleria and Lampedusa in June 1943 and the invasion of Sicily in July, as well as bombing German evacuation beaches near Messina in August. In September the A-20Bs supported the British 8th Army during the invasion of Italy and took part in the Allied advance on Rome from September 1943 to June 1944.

USAF

The B-26B (41-17747 is seen here) began production in May 1942. It had armour plate around the pilots' area and improved armament, and in addition a ventral tunnel gun and a new tail-gun position were added.

USAF

2nd Lieutenant William Zarhrte of Wisconsin manning the flexible nose gun of a 322nd Bomb Group B-26 Marauder. On the B-26B-10 improvements were made to the flying characteristics by adding a taller fin and rudder and increasing the wing area and wing span. The B-26B grew even heavier with the installation of a second nose gun, two blister guns each side of the fuselage below the cockpit and a Martin-Bell power-operated tail gun. Marauders began equipping the 8th Air Force in England in the spring of 1943. However, their second mission, on 17 May 1943, ended in disaster when all eleven B-26s of the 322nd BG failed to return from a low-level strike on Ijmuiden, Holland.

USAF

Captain Jack Tyson, bombardier nose gunner of a B-26B Marauder of the 322nd Bomb Group, 1943. During the summer of 1943 Marauders were switched to a high-level bombing role and late in 1943 all B-26 groups were transferred to the 9th Air Force. Marauders also fought in the Mediterranean theatre with the USAAF.

USAF

The installation of a Convair tail turret in the nose position was a standard measure on B-24D Liberators in the Pacific until the arrival of Liberators with production nose turrets. Here, the Convair turret has been installed in the nose of B-24D *The Green Hornet* of the 7th Bomb Group, 10th Air Force at Fanafuti Island, Ellis Group, in April 1943.

USAF

B-25C-25-NA 42-64758 in early USAAF maritime scheme, one of a hundred built that completed production of the C model at Inglewood, California, in May 1943. It has been retrofitted with a 75-mm M-4 cannon in the lower left side of the forward fuselage below the two fixed .50-calibre nose guns. This cannon was tested in the XB-25G on 22 October 1942 and five B-25C-15s were completed as B-25G-1s, the first flying on 16 March 1943. The M-4 was hand-loaded with twenty-one rounds from the loading tray behind the pilot. The last of 400 B-25C-25s completed as B-25Gs were finished by August 1943.

USAF

B-25G-10-NA 42-65199 on a test flight over southern California before being shipped out to the Pacific for combat operations. The 5th Air Force used the B-25Gs against shipping and ground targets, but the cannons were removed from eighty-two B-25Gs and replaced by two .50-calibre guns in the cannon tunnel, two more in the nose and a pair of .30s in the tail.

USAF

Heavier armament was introduced on the B-25H model (43-4501 *Norma Sue* is seen here), which had a lighter-weight T13E-1 75-mm cannon and four fixed .50-calibre guns in the nose, and four more in blisters on both sides of the fuselage. Twelve .50-calibre guns were carried on the 300 B-25H-1s (only two blisters were mounted on the right), but the remaining blocks, beginning with B-25H-5s and ending with -10s, carried fourteen, with twin package guns on both sides of the nose. The Bendix two-gun dorsal power turret was moved forward to the navigator's compartment, just behind the pilot, to improve the field of fire. Some Hs had their cannon removed in the field and replaced with two piggyback rockets mounted, with another slung on the left side of the nose.

USAF

B-25H 43-4570 on a test flight in California, 1944. On 21 August 1942 1,000 B-25Hs had been ordered and the first H models flew on 31 July 1943. B-25H production ended in July 1944 when North American's Inglewood plant changed over completely to P-51 fighter production.

USAF

Opposite, above: Curtiss P-40M 43-5418. The 'M' began replacing the P-40K on the production lines in November 1942 and 600 were built by early 1943. P-40 production and its engine development underwent numerous design improvements.

via Peter C. Smith

Below: P-40M 44-7318 in flight, 1943. In total, the Curtiss-Wright Corporation built 13,738 Warhawks in 6 main variants for the Allied air forces, the Soviet Union and the Free French.

via Philip Jarrett

A-20 of the 389th Bomb Squadron, 312th Bomb Group is seen in New Guinea, 1944. In US service the 5th Air Force operated the A-20 at masthead height in the Pacific and used the aircraft to excellent effect during the battle for Dutch New Guinea, while the 47th BG of the 12th Air Force used A-20s in the Italian campaign.

via Paul Wilson

Despite its drawbacks the P-38's devastating fire-power and excellent rate of climb earned the respect of its German adversaries, who referred to the P-38 as the 'Fork-Tailed Devil'. The Japanese, also, learned to hate the Lightning. The P-38 destroyed more Japanese aircraft than any other American plane and the two leading American aces, Major Richard Bong and Major Tom McGuire (forty and thirty-eight kills respectively), flew P-38s in the Pacific theatre. In April 1943 P-38Gs of the 339th Fighter Squadron succeeded in intercepting and shooting down the Mitsubishi transport carrying Admiral Yamaoto, mastermind of the Japanese attack on Pearl Harbor. The interception, 550 miles from their base at Guadalcanal, was made possible by the use of long-range drop tanks. Pictured here is a P-38G-10-LO with two 165-US gallon drop tanks and four triple-cluster 4.5-in rocket launchers.

Lockheed

A P-38J at Bassingbourn, Cambridgeshire, early 1944. The P-38J appeared in August 1943 and it began arriving in the UK in February 1944. Lightnings were used mainly to accompany American heavy bombers of the 8th and 15th Air Forces on long-range missions from Britain and Italy respectively. P-38J 42-67032 is seen here.

via Tom Cushing

In North Africa, on 20 July 1943, two 9th Air Force B-24D Liberator Groups, the 98th and 376th, and three 8th Air Force B-24D groups, the 44th, 93rd and 389th, who were on TDY (Temporary Duty) with the 9th, began twelve days' training for 'Tidal Wave'. This was the code name for the low-level bombing raid on the Ploesti oilfields in Romania that took place on 1 August, and involved practice flights against a mock-up target. B-24Ds in small groups crisscrossed the Libyan desert in all directions, until eventually a full-dress rehearsal incorporated the entire force of 175 Liberators.

USAF

A B-24D of the 98th Bomb Group over the Astra Romana refinery, the largest and most modern at Ploesti, amid smoke and flame. The 'Pyramiders' suffered the highest casualties of all 5 groups, losing 21 of the 38 B-24Ds that started out. At least nine were destroyed by the blasts from the delayed action bombs dropped by the 376th BG.

USAF

Opposite, above: Lieutenant-General Lewis H. Brereton, CO 9th Air Force, at an open-air meeting at the 376th 'Liberandos' Bomb Group base at Benghazi spells out the Ploesti mission to crews, August 1943. Brereton warned that losses could reach even as high as 50 per cent. He was of the opinion that if the refineries were demolished and the entire force wiped out, it would still be worth the price.

USAF

Below: B-24D-85-CO 42-40664 *Teggie Ann* of the 515th Bomb Squadron, which carried Brigadier-General Uzal G. Ent, CO 9th Bomber Command, and Colonel Keith K. Compton, CO 376th Bomb Group, to Ploesti and back. Colonel Compton and General Ent had command of this vital mission unexpectedly thrust upon them after the loss of the original lead aircraft just after take-off from North Africa. *Teggie Ann* crash-landed at Melfi, Italy, returning from a raid on Foggia on 16 August 1943.

USAF

The 389th were the last bomb group off from Libya, and Colonel Jack Wood led the twenty-six B-24s of the 'Sky Scorpions' in Major Kenneth 'Fearless' Caldwell's Liberator to their target at 'Red I', Steaua Romana at Campina, the second largest refinery. 'Red' target, seen burning after bombs dropped by the Liberators, was completely destroyed. Five Medals of Honor, three posthumously, were awarded to airmen on this mission, and all five groups received Presidential Unit Citations. Only 42 per cent of the Ploesti oil plants' refining capacity and 40 per cent of the cracking capacity were destroyed on 1 August, for the loss of 57 B-24Ds, while 6 were interned in Turkey and 55 returned with battle damage. Most of the refineries were repaired and within a month were operating at pre-mission capacity again.

USAF

Opposite, above: C-47C 42-5671 was modified into an amphibian by Edo at its Oklahoma City factory by fitting 41-ft long pontoons and a series of watertight bulkheads to carry fuel. Testing of the XC-47C prototype took place at Floyd Bennett Field, New York. It was found that the weight and drag caused by the Edo floats reduced the speed of the aircraft by about 30mph compared with conventional C-47s, and so between July and August 1943 JATO bottles were fitted at Wright Field during tests to improve take-off performance. Just five C-47C floatplanes were built by Douglas for ASR operation in the Pacific and Alaska.

Douglas

Below: A B-24D of the 28th Composite Group, 11th Air Force, taxi-ing along the runway after returning from a raid on Paramushiro, September 1943.

USAF

B-24D Liberator of the 308th Bomb Group taking off at Kunming, China, over the heads of Chinese wagons and parked C-46s and C-47s, 1943.

USAF

Opposite, above: B-24Ds of the 28th Composite Group, 11th Air Force landing in a snow storm in the Aleutian Islands after returning over the Bering Sea from bombing Japanese targets on Kiska and Attu in the western Aleutians, September 1943.

USAF

Below: A Curtiss C-46A Commando and a Curtiss P-40E of the 26th Fighter Squadron, 51st Fighter Group, 14th Air Force, at Kunming, China, 1943. The 51st was at first assigned to the 10th Air Force in March 1942 in India. After defending the Indian terminus of the 'Hump' route and airfields in that area, the Group flew strafing, bombing, reconnaissance and patrol missions in support of the Allied ground troops during a Japanese offensive in northern Burma in 1943. The 51st Fighter Group moved to China in October 1943 and was assigned to the 14th Air Force. Using P-38s and P-40s it defended the eastern end of the route over the 'Hump', guarded air bases in the Kunming area, harassed enemy shipping in the Red River delta and supported Chinese ground forces in their drive along the Salween River.

USAF

Curtiss C-46A Commandos in formation, 1944. The design originated in 1937 as a 36-seat commercial transport, but in the Second World War the C-46 was widely used as a troop and freight carrier for the AAFs. The Commando operated primarily in the Pacific theatre because of its greater load-carrying capability and better performance at high altitude than the C-47. Its most famous theatre of operations was the supply of war material to China from India over the 'Hump'. Altogether, 1,491 C-46s were built and many remained in service after the war.

via Philip Jarrett

B-24 Liberators of the 7th Air Force en route from the Marshalls to Truk, 1944.

USAF

Seemingly unconcerned, British workmen at Great Dunmow, Essex, continue with runway construction as a B-26 Marauder of the 386th Bomb Group (Medium) lifts off. Note that the censor has obliterated the package guns on this photograph of this aircraft.

USAF

Martin B-26F-1-MA 42-96246 TQ-H of the 559th Bomb Squadron, 387th Bomb Group (Medium), 8th Air Force, which transferred to the 9th Air Force in October 1943. The B-26F had the wing incidence angle increased slightly in an effort to further improve take-off performance. Some 300 Fs were built, of which 200 went to the RAF and SAAF, before minor internal changes altered the designation to B-26G. Some 893 Gs were built before deliveries ceased in March 1945. Altogether, 5,266 Marauders were built, of which 1,585 were built in Omaha, Nebraska, and 3,681 in Baltimore.

USAF

The Vultee Model 54 low-wing monoplane (affectionately known as the 'Vibrator') became the most numerous of the basic trainers used in the Second World War. An intial order for 300 was placed with Vultee at Nashville, Tennessee, in 1939, and eventually orders totalling 6,407 BT-13A versions followed. These were followed by an order for 1,125 BT-13B models.

via Philip Jarrett

Opposite, above: AAC cadets march past their PT-17 Stearmans on the flight line at the Twenty-nine Palms Air Academy during the winter of 1943.

Don Downie

Below: The Convair B-32 Dominator was developed as a parallel project to the Boeing B-29 Superfortress as a safeguard against delays in production. Prototypes were ordered in September 1940, ostensibly as replacements for the B-17 and B-24. The first of three XB-32s were flown on 7 September 1942, and the second on 2 July 1943. The third prototype, which was changed from twin- to single-tail, was flown on 9 November 1943. Technical troubles delayed the B-32's introduction into service until 1945, when only fifteen saw limited action in the western Pacific before the end of the war. A total of forty TB-32s were completed as trainers; another 1,588 B-32s were cancelled.

General Dynamics

General Douglas McArthur's B-17E-BO (XC-108) 41-2593 *Bataan*, 29 November 1943. It was one of four B-17E and Fs specially converted into transports under the C-108 designation in 1943. Although an E, *Bataan* had a 'blown' B-17F style Plexiglas nose with a single .50-calibre gun with chromed barrel (the only armament carried) and a navigator's astrodome added to the aircraft. A five-man crew and up to eleven passengers could be carried on the XC-108.

Boeing

Sand-coloured B-25C 42-32304 of the 487th Bomb Squadron, 340th Bomb Group, in the MTO, late 1943.

USAF

Beginning in April 1943 and ending in August 1945, North American produced 4,318 B-25Js, the first flying on 14 December 1943. B-25J 43-3892 is seen here in 1944.

B-25C Mitchells of the 321st Bomb Group (Medium) taxi out at Amandola, Italy, December 1943.

The B-25J became the most widely used of all the Mitchell models, and 42-28844 is seen here. Normal armament was a flexible gun in the nose, with a fixed gun on the right side of the nose, four .50-calibre package guns, two .50-calbre waist guns, two .50-calibre guns in the Bendix upper turret and two .50-calibre guns in a power-operated tail turret. Some Js were modified to carry eight .50-calibre machine-guns in the nose.

USAF

The Vought-Sikorsky Division of United Aircraft produced the first helicopter for the USAAF, the XR-4, which made its first flight on 13 January 1942 powered by a 165hp Warner R-500-3 engine. The USAAF ordered 30 R-4s for further service trials and followed this with a final order for 100 R-4Bs (43-46500/46599).

via Philip Jarrett

Opposite, above: North American B-25D 41-30340 *El Diablo IV*, one of the strafers of the 3rd Attack Group, First Air Task Force, 5th Air Force, over the barren Cape Gloucester landscape, during the battle for New Britain in the Bismarck Archipelago, December 1943. The 3rd Attack Group was composed of one squadron of A-20s and three of B-25 Mitchell strafers.

USAF

Below: UC-43 Traveler (Beech 17) 43-10828 in formation, 18 January 1944. First used by USA embassy attachés to foreign capitals, the UC-43 was widely put into service as an 'aerial workhorse' at many air bases in the USA and Britain during the Second World War.

via Philip Jarrett

On 5 February 1944 Lieutenant Robert Mims' B-26C-22-MA *Swamp Chicken* of the 323rd Bomb Group, which was on its 52nd mission of the war, took a direct flak hit in the right engine over Frèvent, during a shallow penetration mission to France to bomb a V-weapon site. Bombardier John Brush manually salvoed the eight 500-lb bombs after they failed to jettison. Mims gave his co-pilot Lieutenant Leon Jackson the choice of baling out or remaining on board to crash-land the aircraft. He chose the former. Mims held the mangled aircraft as steady as he could while Jackson baled out and then superbly crash-landed the stricken Maruader in a field near a German flak battery. Mims, Brush, Bill Vermillion, radioman, and Sergeant McCandish, a replacement tail gunner on his first mission, were all captured. Engineer Michael Miyo evaded capture, and with the help of the French Underground made it safely across the Pyrenees to Spain. Leon Jackson's chute failed to open and he was killed. The flak barrage that had claimed *Swamp Chicken* also brought down two other 323rd BG B-26s and damaged a further thirty aircraft, one so badly that it was abandoned over their home base after heading it out over the North Sea.

USAF

On 28 February 1944 Lieutenant Frank Remmele flew Ben Willis' (CO 449th Bomb Squadron, 322nd Bomb Group (Medium)) B-26 *Truman Committee* on a mission to a V-weapon site in France. It returned damaged with shell splinters (arrowed) from flak bursts that wounded the pilot and killed the bombardier. On 27 May *Truman Committee*, with Remmele, now a veteran of over sixty combat missions, once again at the controls, was hit by two shell bursts while returning from a Seine bridge attack. The explosions tore away the main fuel gauge and blasted the main fuel cell, the aileron and hydraulic lines in the right wing. Remmele crash-landed the stricken Marauder at the fighter airfield at Friston, and with no flaps and no brakes it careered across the coastal aircraft at 175mph, heading perilously close to the edge of the cliffs and threatened to land in the sea. Remmele only managed to bring *Truman Committee* to a halt by restarting the right engine and swinging the aircraft left into a pill box. The impact ripped off the undercarriage and the B-26 sailed over the top of the pill box before digging its left wingtip into the earth and skidding round to a stop. Remmele and his crew emerged from the wreckage with no lasting injuries.

USAF

B-24H-5-CF 41-29212 of the 720th Bomb Squadron, 450th 'Cottontails' Bomb Group, in the 47th Bomb Wing bellies in at Manduria, Italy, after the left main gear collapsed, 14 March 1944.

USAF

B-26 Marauders near the Alps, early 1944. In February, March and April 1944 the Marauders in the MTO played a major part in Operation 'Strangle', the cutting of all lines of supply that the enemy needed to support the German Army on the Anzio and Cassino fronts. 'They stole the show' was the tribute paid to the Marauders by Lieutenant-General Ira C. Eaker, C-in-C of the Mediterranean Allied Air Force, for the part the B-26s played in the bombardment of Cassino on 15 March 1944.

USAF

Opposite, above: P-38J-5-LO 42-67183 and Azure-blue-finish F-5B-1-LO 42-67332, photographic version, in flight over California, 1943. In total 2,970 P-38Js were produced and they were easily distinguishable by the introduction of 'chin' radiators in the front of the engine nacelles. Some 200 F-5B-1s, essentially converted P-38Js with cameras, were delivered from September to December 1943. The 10th Photo Group of the 9th Air Force used F-5Bs and -Cs from April 1944.

Lockheed

Below: F-5G-6-LO, the last photographic-reconnaissance version of the Lightning, 1944. The F-5G was a P-38L conversion, just as the F-5B was a conversion of the P-38G, the F-5C a conversion of the P-38H and the F-5E a conversion of both the P-38J and P-38L.

Lockheed

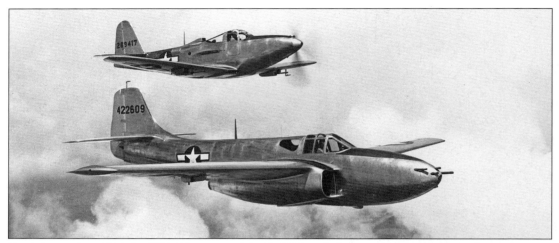

On 5 September 1941 the USAAF requested the Bell Aircraft Corporation to undertake development of a jet-fighter design to take advantage of early British design work on gas-turbine power plants. XP-59A Airacomet construction began in spring 1942 as a mid-wing monoplane with a slender fuselage incorporating two General Electric J-31 turbojets. The XP-59A flew on 1 October 1942 and thirteen YP-59As were delivered during 1944. P-59A 44-22609, seen here with Kingcobra 42-69417, was the first of twenty production Airacomets designated as trainers and armed with one 37-mm cannon and three .50-in machine-guns in the nose. The P-59As were followed by 30 P-59Bs before the contract was cancelled on 30 October 1943 because of the successful development of the P-80. The P-59s were issued to the 412th Fighter Group, a trials unit within the 4th Air Force.

Bell

15th Air Force P-51D Mustangs with wing drop tanks. HL-A is from the 308th Fighter Squadron, 31st Fighter Group; WD-Q is a 4th Fighter Squadron, 52nd Fighter Group machine; No. 7 is from the 332nd Fighter Group and 00 is a 325th Fighter Group P-51D.

USAF

With fifty missions to his credit, Ralph E. Miller of Oklahoma, waist gunner of 41-31919 *Mild and Bitter*, a 322nd Bomb Group (Medium), 9th Air Force, B-26B Marauder, loads his guns in the rear fuselage of the aircraft. On 8 May 1944 *Mild and Bitter* recorded its hundredth mission, having flown its first on 28 July 1943 leading a sweep over Abbeville. Captain Paul Shannon flew the *Mild and Bitter* on its hundredth mission, having been the B-26's original pilot and having piloted it on twenty-seven other sorties. The aircraft was then flown stateside to tour the war factories in the USA.

USAF

B-24s of the 15th Air Force during a raid on the oil refineries at Blechhammer, Germany.

Martin B-26B Marauder 42-959994 *Naomi Elaine* of the 319th Bomb Group (Medium), 12th Air Force, banks away after bombing the Campo Di Marte freight yards at Florence, Italy, 2 May 1944.

USAF

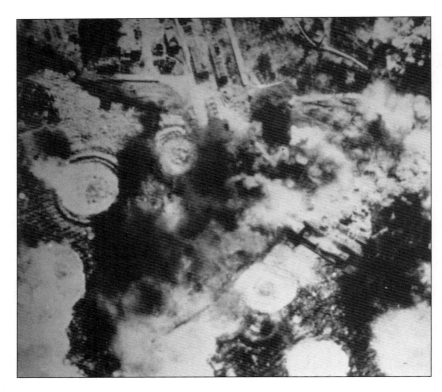

15th Air Force
Liberators bombing
San Stefano, Italy,
15 May 1944.

USAF

15th Air Force Liberators bombing Nice, France, 26 May 1944. Almost 700 15th Air Force heavies attacked marshalling yards in southern France on this day.

USAF

B-24s of the 727th Bomb Squadron, 451st Bomb Group, coming off the bomb run against the Concordia Vega oil refinery at Ploesti, 31 May 1944. Top left is B-24G-5-NT 42-78145 *Con Job*, and right is B-24H-5-CF 41-29233 *The Sod Buster*. *Con Job* and Lieutenant Dick Turnbull's crew failed to return from a raid on Vienna on 22 August 1944, while *The Sod Buster* completed sixty-nine missions before being salvaged on 20 September 1944.

USAF

B-17s of the 15th Air Force attack the Schwechat oil refinery at Vienna, Austria, through thick flak, 1944.

USAF

B-26B Marauders of the 555th Bomb Squadron, 386th Bomb Group (Medium) on their second or third bombing mission on D-Day, 6 June 1944. Leading is B-26B 41-31812 *Mr Five By Five*, which had completed seventy-five missions by July 1944.

USAF

A tight formation of P-61A night-fighters of the 422nd NFS, 9th Air Force, with, centre, 42-5564 *Jukin Judy* with shark's teeth and eye, and, right, 42-5573 with a large heart on the nose. The Northrop P-61 Black Widow was the first aircraft in the world designed from the outset as a night-fighter. Altogether, the P-61 equipped eight squadrons in the Pacific, first going into action with the 6th Night Fighter Squadron, 18th Fighter Group, 13th Air Force, which landed on Saipan on 21 June 1944. The first Black Widow victory was obtained nine days later, and a second on 6 July. During March and June 1944 the 422nd and 425th Night Fighter Squadrons of the 9th Air Force arrived in England equipped with the P-61A.

Merle Olmsted

B-26C Marauder 42-107685 ER-V of the 450th Bomb Squadron, 322nd Bomb Group, 9th Air Force, wearing black and white D-Day stripes. During the summer of 1943 Marauders were switched to a high-level bombing role, but the bomber's success was only finally achieved, late in 1943, when all B-26 groups were transferred to the 9th Air Force for tactical missions in support of the Allied build-up to the invasion of Europe. A total of 1,235 B-26Cs, which were not dissimilar to the B-26B, were built by Martin at Omaha, Nebraska.

USAF

A mix of solid-nosed and Plexiglas-nosed A-20Gs of the 668th Squadron, 416th Bomb Group (Medium), 9th Air Force, D-Day, 6 June 1944.

USAF

Opposite, above: The XCG-17 was an experimental troop-transport glider created in the summer of 1944 at Clinton County Army Base in Ohio by removing the engines and fairing over the nacelles of C-47-DL 41-18496. It flew for the first time in June 1944. The aircraft was later re-engined and delivered to Mavis-Monthan for storage on 25 August 1946. In 1949 the engines were fitted to the nacelles and was sold as N69030 to a commercial operator.

Douglas

Below: B-26B-55-MA 42-96165 of the 599th Bomb Squadron, 397th Bomb Group (Medium), 9th Air Force, with shark's teeth and D-Day invasion stripes. This aircraft was transferred to the 558th Bomb Squadron, 387th BG, shortly before the end of the war.

USAF

P-51Bs and Ds of the 374th
Fighter Squadron,
361st Fighter Group,
8th Air Force, from
Bottisham,
Cambridgeshire, sporting
D-Day stripes and fuselage
drop tanks. The nearest
aircraft is P-51B B7-E 42-
106839 *Bald Eagle*.
via Tom Cushing

Douglas C-47A-DK 42-92099 *Iron Ass* of the 75th Squadron, 435th Troop Carrier Group, 9th Air Force, and B-17G-DL 44-6349 of the 301st Bomb Group, 15th Air Force at Horsham St Faith near Norwich, home base of the 458th Bomb Group, flying Liberators, 1944.

via Jack Krause

Lockheed XP-58 Chain Lightning (41-2670) experimental escort fighter and anti-ship destroyer, one-third larger than the P-38 and equipped with twin tail turrets and four .37-mm high-velocity cannon in the nose. Lack of suitable power plants resulted in the XP-58 not being flown until 6 June 1944, more than four years after design had begun.

Lockheed

B-26B-15 Marauder *Rat Poison*, a veteran of 164 missions, of the 386th Bomb Group (Medium), on the former Luftwaffe airfield at Beaumont, France, 1944. The 386th flew their last Marauder mission in February 1945 but retained this famous B-26 as a group transport after it converted to the A-26 Invader.

USAF

B-26B 42-95930 KX-D of the 558th Bomb Squadron, 387th Bomb Group, 9th Air Force with distinctive yellow and black striped tail.

via Philip Jarrett

B-17G-30-DL 42-38213 (olive drab) and B-17G-35-DL 42-106984 (natural metal finish) at the Douglas Long Beach factory. 42-106984 did not leave the USA, while 42-38213 was assigned to the 20th Bomb Squadron, 2nd Bomb Group, 15th AF, and was lost on 7 July 1944 on the mission to Bleckhammer. Douglas-built G models were the first to become operational, the AAF receiving their first G on 4 September 1943. Leaving the bomber unpainted speeded up production and increased overall flight performance. Douglas built 2,395 G models.

Douglas

B-17G-25-DL 42-38069 and other Gs of the 49th Bomb Squadron, 2nd Bomb Group, are seen returning to Italy from Blechhammer, Germany, 7 July 1944. They are accompanied by a P-38 Lightning that was hit by flak over the target area and has its starboard engine feathered. 42-38069 was lost on the mission to Odertal, Germany, on 22 August 1944.

USAF

B-26 Marauder *Josephine II* of the 438th Bomb Squadron, 319th Bomb Group, makes a diving turn off the target to evade flak as a road bridge in the Po Valley in Italy disintegrates, 1944. The 319th boasted several Marauder centenarians, including *Hell's Belle II*, the first B-26 to notch up 100 missions in all theatres, when it returned from a raid on Florence on May Day 1944.

USAF

B-24 Liberator of the 465th Bomb Group, 15th Air Force, en route to attack a target in southern Germany, summer, 1944.

USAF

Opposite, above: B-24D-50-CO 42-40323 *Frenesi* of the 370th Bomb Squadron, 307th Bomb Group (note the 'Long Rangers' on the tail), 13th Air Force, a veteran of 110 missions, on Los Negros, July 1944. The A-6 tail-turret installation in the nose is a result of a field modification at the Hawaiian Air Depot where this was also the first B-24 to have a ball turret retrofitted.

USAF

Below: A 376th Bomb Group B-24 having lost part of the wing to flak over Toulon, France. The port was hit repeatedly by heavy bombers of the 15th Air Force during the early part of 1944 and up until 20 August 1944 as part of the softening up process for the 'Anvil' invasion.

USAF

Combat photographer Sergeant Leo S. Stoutsenberger captured the demise of the 725th Bomb Squadron, 451st Bomb Group, deputy leadship, B-24H-30-FO 42-95379 *Extra Joker*, flown by Lieutenant Ken A. Whiting, on the mission to Markersdorf airfield, Vienna, 23 August 1944. As the formation reached the IP (Initial Point) at 22,000 ft the Group was attacked by numerous Fw 190s and *Extra Joker* (it was given this name after a playing card was found aboard on delivery to the group) was hit by cannon fire in the main fuel tanks which spread through the flight deck and waist. The B-24 fell out of formation and slowly spiralled down some 5,000 ft before exploding at 11.16 hours near Turnitz, Austria. Lieutenant Whiting and his crew were lost. Lack of fighter escort was cited as the chief cause of the high losses sustained over Austria on 22 and 23 August. The 451st, which over the two days lost fifteen Liberators and two more so badly damaged that they had to be written off, was awarded a DUC – its third – for this mission.

USAF

A-20 Havocs of the 669th Bomb Squadron, 416th Bomb Group, 9th Air Force. After supporting the invasion in June 1944 by striking at road junctions, marshalling yards, bridges and railway overpasses, the group assisted ground forces at Caen and St Lô in July. During the enemy's retreat through the Falaise Gap, 6–9 August 1944, the 416th BG bombed several targets despite heavy resistance and were awarded a DUC for their actions. In November the group converted to the A-26 Invader.

USAF

Waco CG-4A troop-carrying gliders with D-Day markings landing at a rough strip near the Normandy beachhead, June/July 1944. The CG-4A could carry thirteen troops. Cessna Aircraft of Wichita, Kansas, was selected to build 750 Waco CG-4A gliders but the company subcontracted the entire order to the Wichita Division of Boeing, who literally built them in the aisles of the new Plant 2 while tooling up for Superfortress production.

USAF

Deadly Nightshade. P-61B 42-39728 in the traditional gloss-black overall scheme, characteristic of later Black Widow models. In August 1944 the first of 450 P-61B models appeared. The 'B' made provison for increased loads and, after modifications had eliminated the buffeting problems associated with the earlier turret, 200 models, from P-61B-15 to P-61B-20, had the dorsal turret restored. The P-61B-10 could carry four 1,600-lb bombs or 165- or 300-gallon drop tanks below the wings. Despite its size, the Black Widow was a highly manouevrable aircraft, with retractable laminar flow ailerons and lateral-control spoilers allowing fast, tight turns to out-turn an F6F Hellcat and give even the Spitfire a run for its money.

Northrop

B-26C of the 496th Bomb Squadron, 344th Bombardment Group (Medium) bombing enemy targets on the continent, 1944. The Group received a DUC for a three-day action against the enemy, 24–6 July 1944, when the Group struck at targets assisting the advance on St Lô.

USAF

B-26B-40-MA Marauder 42-43304 *Marlin* of the 444th Bomb Squadron, 320th Bomb Group (Medium), 9th Air Force.

USAF

B-24s of the 465th Bomb Group leaving the target, two marshalling yards at Hatvan, Hungary, 20 September 1944. On this day, apart from the attacks on Hatvan, almost 500 B-24s and B-17s, escorted by P-38s and P-51s, bombed three rail bridges at Budapest, a marshalling yard at Gyor, as well as the airfield at Malacky and the oil district at Bratislava.

USAF

Opposite, above: Lockheed P-38L-5-LO 44-25419. The L was the final production version of the Lightning and first appeared in June 1944. By August 1945 2,520 were built at Burbank, California. A contract for 2,000 P-38L-VNs, which had been ordered on 26 June 1944 from Consolidated-Vultee at Nashville, was cancelled after just 113 had been received by June 1945.

Lockheed

Below: Republic P-47D Thunderbolt 42-26463. The P-47C was replaced on the production lines on 14 October 1941 by the first of 850 P-47Ds. A further 1,050 Ds were to be built at a new Republic factory at Evansville, Indiana, from the end of January 1942. The first P-47Ds retained the old-style canopy but from P-47D-25 on Thunderbolts were fitted with a 'teardrop' moulded cockpit hood for improved rearward vision. Altogether, some 12,602 Ds were built. Water injection was used in the R-2800-21 and later R-2800-59 engines which powered the P-47D model to boost engine power at higher altitudes.

USAF

Republic P-47D Thunderbolts of the 350th Fighter Group, 12th Air Force, late in 1944.

USAF

B-24 of the 460th Bomb Group with evidence of tail damage sustained during a raid on Munich on 22 September 1944. Some 366 B-24s and B-17s, escorted by 270 fighters, bombed the north-east industrial area of the Bavarian capital as well as the Munich-Riem jet airfield.

USAF

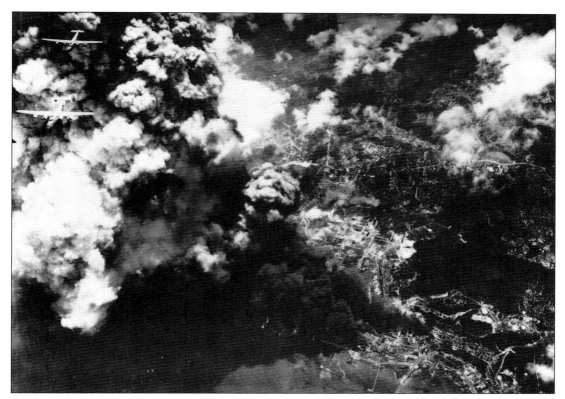

In September 1944 the 5th Air Force, as part of the New Guinea campaign, began flying missions against the oil refineries at Balikpapan in Borneo. This refinery was known as the 'Ploesti of the Pacific' and only second in production to Palembang in Sumatra. The first raid on the Balikpapan oilfields had been made by B-24s of the 380th Bomb Group on 13 August 1943 in a 17-hour sortie from Darwin, Australia. Two further raids were made, and in September 1944 the airfield at Noemfoor in north-west New Guinea became available, reducing the flying time to 14 hours and allowing the B-24s to carry a 2,500-lb bomb load.

via Elmer Vogel

A 7th Bomb Group B-24 leaving the Blin rail bridge in Burma, November 1944.

USAF

Its tail knocked off in a mid-air collision with B-24 42-52045 *Burma Bell* from the 726th Bomb Squadron, 451st Bomb Group, flown by Lieutenant Shelton, Lieutenant Theodore King's B-24 42-51941, also from the 726th, dives to earth just after bombs away at the synthetic oil and coking plant at Ordertal near Blechhammer, Germany, on 17 December 1944. None of King's crew survived, and the co-pilot of *Burma Bell* was killed in the collision.

USAF

B-26Gs of the 456th Bomb Squadron, 323rd Bomb Group, 9th Air Force, dropping bombs over enemy occupied Europe, 1944. This group flew its first night mission after moving to the continent in August 1944, and received a DUC for action between 24 and 27 December 1944 during the Battle of the Bulge.

USAF

A fleet of C-109 'Flying tankers' operated by Air Transport Command in India, used to support B-29 operations in the CBI, 1944. All C-109s were conversions of B-24J and L models with the turrets deleted, and were fitted with seven specially designed fuel tanks in the bomb bay, and one more in the nose, to give a fuel-carrying capacity of 2,900 US gallons.

USAF

B-29s on the ramps outside Seattle Plant 2 late in the war. Since early in 1942 the plant had been concealed with a camouflage hill, complete with city housing, streets and cars.

Boeing

Opposite, above: B-26G-55-MA 44-67835 of the 586th Bomb Squadron, 394th Bomb Group (Medium), 9th Air Force, 1944.

USAF

Below: B-24J Liberator of the 11th Bomb Group, 7th Air Force, overflies the swaying palms of Makin Island.

USAF

B-29A-BN 42-93844, with both sets of bomb-bay doors open, 1944. Renton-built articles differed only in having four guns instead of two in the front turret.

Boeing

Opposite, above: B-24 *Dual Sack* of the 7th Air Force just above the Ocean off the formidable coastline of Japanese Chichi Jima on a Bonin Island shipping raid. Regular Liberator shipping strikes helped to keep the Japanese bottled up north of the Marianas, and ease resistance for the Superfortresses.

USAF

Below: B-29s in the 500th VHBG, in Brigadier-General O'Donnell's 73rd Bomb Wing (the second B-29 wing to be formed), dropping bombs on Japan. The 500th VHBG (Very Heavy Bomb Group) became operational on 11 November 1944. During the summer months five B-29 bases were constructed in the newly captured Marianas where it was decided to concentrate all B-29s of XX Air Force. It was from here on 24 November 1944 that the first raid on Tokyo took place when the 73rd Wing bombed the Musashima aircraft factory.

USAF

Ace of aces. Major Richard Ira 'Dick' Bong received the Medal of Honor from General Douglas McArthur on 12 December 1944. The top-scoring American fighter ace with forty victories, Bong was killed flying a P-80A on 6 August 1945.

USAF

B-26B-30-MA Marauder *Bar Fly* of the 554th Bomb Squadron, 396th Bomb Group, flew 175 missions until an engine failed on take-off on New Year's Day 1945. Lieutenant Altenburger's crew escaped without injury, but *Bar Fly* was damaged beyond economical repair.

USAF

Republic P-47D Thunderbolts of the 365th Fighter Group. The 365th had moved to Britain in December 1943 and began combat operations with the 9th Air Force in February 1944. After D-Day the Group moved to the continent where they continued to dive-bomb targets. In September 1944 the 365th flew patrols in co-operation with airborne operations in Holland and were awarded a DUC for destroying and damaging numerous enemy fighters over the Bonn-Dusseldorf area in Germany on 21 October.

USAF

Douglas A-26B 41-39186 of the 533rd Bomb Squadron, 386th Bomb Group (Medium), which converted to the Invader shortly after the Ardennes Campaign between December 1944 and January 1945. It was planned to replace all other mediums with the A-26 Invader and on 10 July 1942 the XA-26 flew for the first time. The first A-26B Invaders became operational in November 1944 with the 9th Air Force in Europe. It proved the fastest American attack plane of the Second World War, with a top speed of 355mph, and packed no fewer than twenty-two guns. A-26Bs normally carried six nose-mounted guns, four blister guns on the fuselage sides and eight guns in four optional underwing pods, as well as two top turret and two belly guns.

USAF

Republic P-47D Thunderbolt
44-20571 D5-C of the
386th Fighter Squadron, 365th
Fighter Group, 9th Air Force, at
Metz, France, winter 1944.
The 365th FG began combat
operations with the 9th Air Force in
February 1944, moving to France
late in June that year where its
P-47s continued to dive-bomb
targets during the succeeding weeks
of the battle for Normandy. In July
the group bombed targets near
St Lô to assist Allied forces in
breaking through German lines at
that point, and supported the
subsequent drive across northern
France during August–September.
In September the 365th FG also
flew patrols in co-operation with
airborne operations in Holland.
On 30 January 1945 the 365th FG
moved to Florennes/Juzaine,
Belgium, remaining there until
16 March when its P-47s moved to
Aachen, Germany. Cited by the
Belgian government for assisting
Allied armies in the period from the
invasion of Normandy through the
initial phases of the liberation of
Belgium, the group received a
second Belgian award for actions
during the Battle of the Bulge. The
group finished the war with two
DUC awards.

USAF

B-24s of the 460th Bomb Group dropping fragmentation bombs on the airfield at Neuberg, Austria, 26 March 1945. Over 500 heavies escorted by P-51s and P-38s bombed marshalling yards at Wiener-Neustadt and other targets in Austria, Czechoslovakia and Hungary.

USAF

B-24J-180-CO 44-40759 *Shack Bunny* of the 867th Bomb Squadron, 494th Bomb Group, over the Gulf of Java en route to Japanese targets at Mintal aerodrome on Mindanao in the Philippines, March 1945.

USAF

Republic P-47Ns, 1945. The final version of the Thunderbolt was built solely for escorting B-29s in the Pacific and consequently the N had the greatest range of all P-47 models. A wing of 18 in greater span was strengthened to accommodate two 93-gallon tanks internally in addition to two drop tanks. P-47Ns began arriving in the Pacific in 1945 where their 2,350-mile range made them ideal for B-29 escort duty in the final stages of the war.

via Philip Jarrett

Another late arrival in the Pacific before the end of the war was the P-38M two-seat Night-Lightning (P-38M-5-LO 44-27234 is seen here), seventy-five of which were built from existing P-38L airframes. The P-38M was equipped with a SCR540 radar in a nose radome operated by an observer in a raised seat behind the pilot. In addition to the two 20-mm cannon and four .50-in machine-gun armament retained from the P-38L, the Night-Lightning also had launching racks for HVAR rockets beneath the wing.

Lockheed

B-29 *Censored* in the 39th VHBG, which became operational on 6 April 1945, taxies out at North Field, Guam, 1945. Despite an effective blockade and relentless bombing by an ever-increasing number of B-29s – by April 1945 Major-General Curtis E. LeMay, Commanding General XXI Bomber Command, had 4 wings and up to 700 Superfortresses under his command – Japan refused to surrender. Throughout early 1945 B-29s based on Saipan, Tinian and Guam made intensive raids on the Japanese mainland, her environs and oil refineries. For attacks on the refineries B-29s in the 315th BW based on Guam were stripped of all armament except the tail turret, and AN/APQ-7 'Eagle' radar bomb sights were installed. Another unit, the 313th, carried out highly successful aerial mining of Japanese home waters and shipping lanes. The 39th flew their first mission, to Maug, in the northern Marianas, early in April 1945.

USAF

Grey pathfinder ship B-24L-10-FO 44-49710 *Stevonovitch II* of the 779th Bomb Squadron, 464th Bomb Group, takes a direct hit between the number 1 and 2 engines from the fourth Flak burst to explode near the Group formation, just after 'bombs away' and goes down on Operation 'Wowser', the mission in support of ground troops near Lugo, Italy, on 10 April 1945. The aircraft took its name from the son of the 779th Squadron Commander, Colonel James Gilson, who was killed. Only Lieutenant Edward P. Walsh, the Mickey operator, who was thrown clear, survived from the eleven-man crew. Just under three weeks later the war in Europe would be over. The final irony was that this was supposed to be a 'milk run,' so men who were about to finish their missions were sent along.

USAF

B-26B-20-MA Marauder 41-31773 *Flak Bait* of the 449th Bomb Squadron, 322nd Bomb Group (Medium), flying its 200th mission on 18 April 1945 in the hands of Captain William G. Fort, on his eighty-fifth mission, and Colonel John S. Samuel, who had flown seventy-one missions. It is accompanied here by B-26G-5-MA 43-34371. The aptly named *Flak Bait* was said to have received 900 shell and bullet holes by this time. It went on to fly two more missions, its 202nd and last on the 322nd Bomb Group's final raid of the war on 24 April when 1st Lieutenant Warren Langar piloted the plane on the mission to an oil depot at Schrobenhausen.

USAF

F-7A 2-F *Photo Fanny* of the 2nd Photographic Charting Squadron (which was attached to the Far East Air Forces), flown by 1st Lieutenant Steward BeBow, on Palawan, Philippine Islands, 22 July 1945 (where the unit moved, on 5 May, from Morotai). The window in the lower part of the nose is a camera port and the mission symbols are cameras. Note the RC-108 blind landing and SCR-729 antenna system. While on Palawan the F-7As carried out photo-recce flights over Singapore for the USN.

USAF

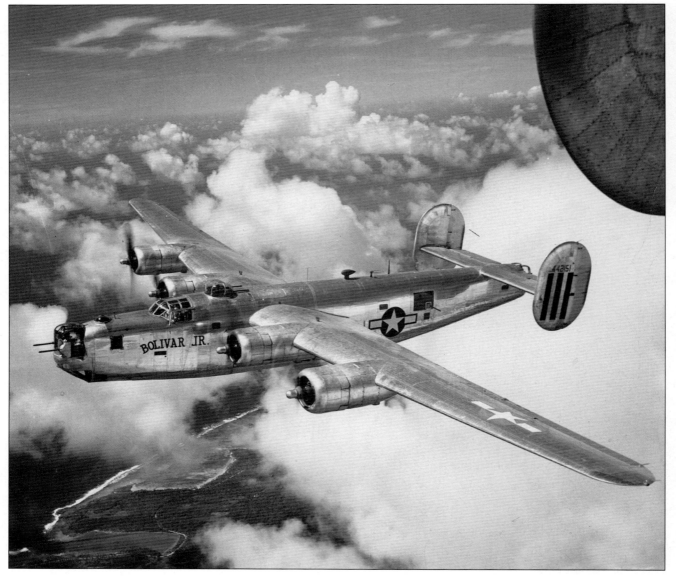

B-24M-20-CO 44-42151 *Bolivar Jr* of the 431st Bomb Squadron, 11th Bomb Group, Mariana Islands, June 1945.

USAF

Opposite above: Douglas A-26B-DL Invader 41-39456 with six .50-inch machine-guns in the nose and remote-controlled dorsal and ventral turrets, 1945. Eight more guns could be added – two each side of the nose and four under the wings. The A-26 flew its final mission in Europe on 3 May 1945, when 130 A-26s of the 9th Air Force, led by PFF Marauders, bombed the Stod Ammon Plant in Czechoslovakia. Only six A-26 groups were in service overseas by August 1945. In the Pacific they were operated by the 3rd Bomb Group in the 5th Air Force and the 319th Bomb Group in the 7th Air Force until 12 August 1945.

USAF

Below: Some 2,000 lightweight P-51H Mustangs, the final production version, were ordered, but only 555 were completed and only a few reached the Pacific theatre before the end of hostilities. P-51H 44-64164 is seen here.

North American

B-17G-5-VE models on the assembly line at Lockheed's Burbank factory, 1944. On 29 July 1945 the last of 8,680 B-17Gs to roll off the Vega assembly line was accepted by the USAAF to bring the grand total of Fortresses built by the BVD (Boeing-Vega-Douglas) pool to 12,731.

Lockheed-California

On 16 July 1945 scientists test-exploded the first atomic device at Alamogordo in the New Mexican desert. President Harry Truman authorized the use of the atomic bomb and a mission directive was sent to General Carl A. Spaatz, Commander of the newly formed US Strategic Air Forces in the Pacific. The 393rd Bomb Squadron, 509th Composite Group, was ready with fifteen specially modified B-39s in the 313th Wing, XXI BC on Tinian, ready to deliver the first atomic bomb, codenamed 'Little Boy', after 3 August 1945 as soon as weather would permit visual bombing. A list of targets was issued to XXI BC: Hiroshima, Kokura, Niigata and Nagasaki. Hiroshima was selected and the mission was set for 6 August. Lieutenant-Colonel Paul Tibbets, Commander of the 509th Composite Group, seen here, took control of the attacking B-29. He had directed that his mother's name, 'Enola Gay', be painted beneath the pilot's cabin on the port side of the fuselage.

USAF

Altogether, seven B-29s were used on the mission, including a reserve aircraft, three weather reconnaissance B-29s and two special-observation aircraft, Major Charles Sweeney's *The Great Artiste*, and Captain George Marquardt's *Necessary Evil*. 'Little Boy' was released from the bomb bay of *Enola Gay* at a height of 31,600 ft and in 43 seconds Hiroshima ceased to exist. The destruction was on an unprecedented scale. Some 48,000 buildings were destroyed and 78,000 Japanese died immediately in the explosion (in the first great B-29 fire-raid against Tokyo, 80,000 had died).

USAF

By 8 August President Truman had still not received any official reaction from the Japanese government so he gave the go ahead for a second atomic device to be dropped on Japan. Kokura was selected as the primary target with Nagasaki as the alternative. Major Charles W. Sweeney, command pilot, used B-29 *Bock's Car*, named after its Commander, Captain Frederick C. Bock, to drop 'Fat Man', a plutonium device and the only remaining atomic weapon in existence, on Nagasaki, Japan, on 9 August 1945 after the primary target was obscured by smoke. An estimated 35,000 people died immediately in the conflagration. The Japanese government surrendered five days later, on 14 August, when a record 804 B-29s bombed targets in Japan. The official surrender ceremony took place aboard the USS *Missouri* in Tokyo Bay on September 2. By then the B-29s had substituted bombs for food supplies and clothing parcels as the majority of these aircraft flew mercy missions to thousands of beleaguered Allied prisoners of war scattered throughout the crumbling Japanese empire.

(Charles W. Sweeney)

INDEX